Poststructuralism
& International Relations

◇

Critical Perspectives
on World Politics

———— ◇ ————

R. B. J. Walker, Series Editor

Poststructuralism & International Relations

Bringing the Political Back In

Jenny Edkins

LYNNE
RIENNER
PUBLISHERS

BOULDER
LONDON

Published in the United States of America by
Lynne Rienner Publishers, Inc.
1800 30th Street, Boulder, Colorado 80301
www.rienner.com

and in the United Kingdom by
Lynne Rienner Publishers, Inc.
3 Henrietta Street, Covent Garden, London WC2E 8LU

Library of Congress Cataloging-in-Publication Data
Edkins, Jenny.
  Poststructuralism and international relations : bringing the
political back in / Jenny Edkins.
      p.   cm. — (Critical perspectives on world politics)
  Includes bibliographical references.
  ISBN 978-1-55587-845-0 (hc : alk. paper)
  1. International relations—Political aspects. 2. International
relations—Philosophy. I. Title. II. Series.
JZ1251.P35   1999
327.1'01—dc21   99-21481
                                                              CIP

British Cataloguing in Publication Data
A Cataloguing in Publication record for this book
is available from the British Library.

Printed and bound in the United States of America

The paper used in this publication meets the requirements
of the American National Standard for Permanence of
Paper for Printed Library Materials Z39.48-1992.

For David

Contents

Tables and Figures

Tables

Figures

Preface

In many areas of social and political theory, the political is being rethought in and through poststructuralist, deconstructivist, feminist, postcolonial, and psychoanalytic thought. In international relations the value of this series of approaches to questions of the political remains widely contested. This book aims both to introduce the interested reader to some of the writings that form the basis for this rethinking and to indicate how it is not only relevant but central to an analysis of politics and the political.

The rethinking of the political that is taking place in contemporary theory (and that has indeed been taking place for some time) involves an unsettling of the view of the "subject" of politics. At one time the political subject was assumed to be the sovereign individual, preexisting politics itself. This concept of the subject has been decentered and the notions of existence and temporality on which it was founded problematized. The unsettling of the subject (of theory as well as of politics) has taken place in parallel with a freeing of the colonized subject, albeit still within a postcolonial world, and a reexamination of boundaries of various kinds constructed to keep subjects in their place.

The challenge to international relations comes not only from a realignment and reexamination of subjectivity that leads to a rearticulation of fundamental political questions but also from a reassessment of "the political" itself. If the unsettled subject can no longer be seen simply as friend or enemy, what is "the political" about? If the boundary between the international and the domestic is insecure in more than the traditional sense, can we still draw the line between politics within and anarchy without? Or is the political moment over once the frontier is in place? As we shall see in Chapter 1, a reassessment of what we might mean by these terms leads a number of writers to make a distinction between "politics" and "the political." It also leads to an analysis that acknowledges the importance of questions of language, discourse, and ideology to a consideration of the political. Much of what we call "politics" is in many senses "depoliticized" or technologized: the room for real political change has been displaced by a technology of expertisc or the rule of bureaucracy.

This book provides an introduction to the work of Jacques Derrida, Michel Foucault, Jacques Lacan, and Slavoj Žižek, among others. These writers provide the tools for the rearticulation of the question of the political. They do this, first, by indicating how what we call "politics" has become depoliticized and technologized and, second, by providing some preliminary notions about what a rethinking of the political or a renegotiation of the boundaries of politics might look like.

In the discipline of international relations, poststructuralist writers continue to be grouped together and their work represented as either apolitical or disengaged. That representation extends to scholars who draw on poststructuralist or psychoanalytic work but locate themselves as dissidents within the disciplines of politics and international relations, as well as to those who draw on a feminist starting point, and it is in part a strategy of marginalization. For its critics, "postmodernism" and its exponents either are irresponsibly pluralistic and lacking in standpoint or their work is so unrelated to what we call "the real world" as to be devoid of any useful application. This book demonstrates that, on the contrary, it is precisely in these writings that we find the possibility of "the political" once again being examined and a series of ways of analyzing and contesting the depoliticization or technologization inherent in "politics" explored.

* * *

I would like to thank colleagues within and beyond the discipline of international relations for help and support at different times and my students, graduate and undergraduate, for their engagement with and enjoyment of the ideas presented here. The Aberystwyth Post-International Group provided inspiration and companionship in the early stages of this project, as did discussions following the British International Studies Association conference in York and at the Sovereignty and Subjectivity Conference in Aberystwyth. Particular thanks go to John Edkins, Véronique Pin-Fat, and Steve Smith. I am grateful to the Leverhulme Trust and the Economic and Social Research Council of the UK for awards that made the research for the book possible. I have a hidden debt to St. Anne's College, Oxford, through whose intransigence I escaped an early depoliticization, and a more obvious one to Stuart Hall, whose inspired teaching at the Open University continues to motivate and inform my work.

Jenny Edkins

1

Politics, Subjectivity, and Depoliticization

This chapter sets out the basic framework within which the claim of the book is situated: the claim that in the writings of poststructuralists, deconstructivists, and psychoanalytic thinkers we find tools that enable us to analyze the political and bring it back into the study of the international. In order to make it clear what I am arguing here, it is necessary first to examine what is meant by notions such as "politics" and "depoliticization" and how they relate to my subsequent analysis of the writings of Foucault, Derrida, Lacan, and Žižek on subjectivity and ideology.

I begin by exploring in a very preliminary way the distinction between "politics" and "the political," terms I use throughout the book. This separation has been discussed by a number of writers—Ernesto Laclau, Philippe Lacoue-Labarthe, Claude Lefort, and Jean-Luc Nancy among them.[1] Michael Dillon has made use of the same differentiation in his reading of Martin Heidegger in relation to security in international politics.[2] I do not go into the complexities of the surrounding disputes about the political and politics in modernity; there is a growing debate on these issues elsewhere.[3] My aim is simply to clarify how I use the terms. The distinction between "politics" and "the political" can be linked with Max Weber's work on politics and bureaucracy.[4] I contend that following Žižek's work, this differentiation can be related to notions of subjectivity, and I show how "the political" implicates and produces subjectivity.[5]

Ironically, what we call "politics" is an area of activity that in modern Western society is "depoliticized" or "technologized." These two terms are more or less synonymous (as far as my usage here goes), but the latter is perhaps more useful as a term because of the sense it conveys that what is going on is something positive. We are not talking about an absence of the political through some sort of lapse or mistake but an express operation of depoliticization or technologization: a reduction to calculability. In this context ideology is the move that conceals the depoliticization of politics

1

and hides the possibility—the risks—of "the political." Technologization has its dangers, too, and one of the fields where its perils can be seen is international politics. As examples, I examine briefly the technologization of famine relief and the notion of securitization as a form of extreme depoliticization. In the final section of this chapter, I outline how the authors whose work I discuss later in the book see processes of technologization and depoliticization.

POLITICS AND THE POLITICAL

The distinction I employ here between "politics" and "the political" is similar to that between what is sometimes called a "narrow" meaning of the political and a broader one. In the narrow sense, the political is taken to be that sphere of social life commonly called "politics": elections, political parties, the doings of governments and parliaments, the state apparatus, and in the case of "international politics," treaties, international agreements, diplomacy, wars, institutions of which states are members (such as the United Nations), and the actions of statesmen and -women. As James Donald and Stuart Hall point out, what gets to be counted as politics in this narrow form is not in any sense given. It is the result of contestation. It is ideological, contingent on a particular organization of the social order, not natural.[6] Donald and Hall refer to the struggle in the 1970s and 1980s by the women's movement to extend the range of politics to include, for example, relations of power within the home or between men and women more broadly. "The personal is political" was their slogan. A similar extension of international politics has been advocated by Cynthia Enloe, this time with the phrase "the personal is international."[7] In other words, the question of what gets to count as "politics" (in the narrow sense) is part of "the political" (in the broader sense): It is a political process. Or in Fred Dallmayr's words, "Whereas politics in the narrower sense revolves around day-to-day decision making and ideological partisanship . . . "the political" refers to the frame of reference within which actions, events, and other phenomena acquire political status in the first place."[8]

In the broader sense, then, "the political" has to do with the establishment of that very social order which sets out a particular, historically specific account of what counts as politics and defines other areas of social life as *not* politics. For Claude Lefort, the political is concerned with the "constitution of the social space, of the form of society."[9] It is central to this process that the act of constitution is immediately concealed or hidden: Hence, "the political is . . . revealed, not in what we call political activity, but in the double movement whereby the mode of institution of society appears and is obscured."[10]

How does this relate to the link that is generally made between "power" and the political? Following Lefort again, "the phenomenon of power lies at the centre of political analysis," but this is not because relations of power should be seen as autonomous and automatically defining "politics." Rather, it is because "the existence of a power capable of obtaining generalised obedience and allegiance implies *a certain type of social division and articulation,* as well as a certain type of representation . . . concerning the legitimacy of the social order."[11] In other words, what is important about power is that it *establishes* a social order and a corresponding form of legitimacy. Power, for Lefort, does not "exist" in any sort of naked form, before legitimation: Rather, the ideological processes of legitimation produce certain representations of power. For a political analysis, in the broadest sense, what needs to be called into question are the conditions of possibility that produced or made conceivable this particular representation of power. The question is, "What change in the principles of legitimacy, what reshaping of the system of beliefs, in the way of apprehending reality, enabled such a representation of power to emerge?"[12]

In any formation of a new state, there are clearly events that would be described as part of "politics" in the narrow sense of the word that are nevertheless significant. But these maneuvers taking place in "politics" do not provide an account in themselves of how one social form rather than another emerges from a period of contestation and struggle. To achieve an understanding of the latter, we need a "political" analysis that examines mutations of the social or symbolic order and how a new model of society is created. In the case of the move to totalitarianism in the USSR, for example, Lefort argues that key to the whole process is that *at the level of fantasy* "what is being created is the model of a society which seems to institute itself without divisions, which seems to have mastery of its own organization, a society in which each part seems to be related to every other and imbued by one and the same project of building socialism."[13] In other words, what is significant in the examination of totalitarianism is how a new symbolic ideal of society, with forms of legitimation, was instituted, and how this model works as fantasy. An analysis of "the political" in the broader sense would involve an account of how such models of the social are articulated and how they work.

Žižek summarizes the distinction made by Lefort and Laclau as one

> between "politics" as a separate social complex, a positively determined sub-system of social relations in interaction with other sub-systems (economy, forms of culture . . .) and the "Political" [*le politique*] as the moment of openness, of undecidability, when the very structuring principle of society, the fundamental form of social pact, is called into question—in short, the moment of global crisis overcome by the act of founding a "new harmony."[14]

Once it is decided (by wars, revolutions, and the like) that legitimate authority resides, for example, with a particular state form, what follows is the bureaucratic technique of governance elaborated through recognized expertise and endorsed in the continuance of the state form through the regular, ritual replacement of the placeholders of authority, whether by elections in a democracy or through the rules of succession in a monarchy or dictatorship. As Max Weber has argued, bureaucracy succeeds because of its technical efficiency, and once in place it is difficult to remove.[15] It replaces the need for political decisions: Actions can be determined on purely technical grounds.

Weber distinguishes between legal rational authority and traditional authority on the one hand, both of which operate according to rules and norms, and charismatic authority on the other. It is the latter that is the province of the political leader, one who takes "politics as a vocation." Weber's contrast between the work of the political leader and that of the bureaucrat or civil servant has many parallels with the distinction between "politics" and "the political" that I am making here. He defines politics as any kind of independent leadership in action, or, more particularly, "the leadership of a political association."[16] The latter is a relation of domination supported by the legitimate (that is, accepted as legitimate) use of force or violence: The means peculiar to the "political" is the use of physical force. In the modern world, the political association is the state, and politics by Weber's definition becomes "striving to share power or striving to influence the distribution of power, either among states or among groups within a state."[17] The political leader has to take responsibility for decisions in a way that the civil servant or administrator does not, and this involves "impossible" choices.[18] Unlike legal rational or traditional authority, political leadership as charismatic authority involves an ethics that cannot be simply an ethic of ultimate ends or an ethic of responsibility but a fusion of the two. It is in one sense an ethic of decision: Once the decision has been taken, there is no other response than that of the person or subject produced in that process: "Here I stand; I can do no other."[19] Political leadership, "politics as a vocation," or charismatic authority would be what I have called here "the political"; the bureaucracy attendant on legal rational authority, in contrast, would be "politics." Weber points out how charismatic authority cannot persist, becoming routinized, or, in our terms, depoliticized:

> In its pure form charismatic authority has a character specifically foreign to everyday routine structures. . . . Indeed, in its pure form, charismatic authority may be said to exist only in the process of originating. It cannot remain stable, but becomes either traditionalized or rationalized, or a combination of both.[20]

The legal rational authority upon which modern bureaucracy depends has no legitimacy beyond the legal system upon which the state's existence relies; the establishment of the legal system itself can claim no transcendent foundation. However, this foundation is provided by myth or ideology. As both Derrida and Žižek point out, once the state is in place, the violence that is involved in its foundation as a particular, historic form is forgotten; the state retroactively constitutes the basis for its own authority. What takes place thereafter, within the state apparatus, is not "the political," but a technology of governance. Ironically, this technology is what we call "politics." It claims to be following the law and legal rational systems of authority; its legitimacy and efficacy are assured only as long as the tenuousness of its claim to sovereign power remains hidden and unchallenged.

As feminists in particular have reminded us,[21] the political is not limited to the grand moments of openness or undecidability that arise in between established social systems, where the whole system of legitimacy previously in place has been effectively challenged and a new one not yet installed. It also arises in the undecidability that is found in every moment of decision, since such moments, as Derrida argues, are not guaranteed by law, technology, or custom.[22] They occur when an act takes place that both reinstates and follows the law. The act of decision is a matter of a specific historical moment; it cannot be justified by an appeal to a general law. Each such act both applies and institutes the law. Once the act, or moment of decision, is past, it disappears: Even the fact that it has taken place cannot be confirmed. The law appears retrospectively merely to have been followed. The political comprises in this sense an interminable process of decisioning, of traversing the undecidable, of faithfulness to what Derrida calls the "double contradictory imperative."[23]

In Laclau's terminology, this moment is the "moment of antagonism."[24] Laclau contrasts social forms, whose origin is concealed (and of which "politics" would be one) with "the political": "The social world presents itself to us, primarily, as a sedimented ensemble of social practices accepted at face value, without questioning the founding acts of their institution."[25] For Laclau, however, the social world is not closed or complete but structured around a lack. Social order is characterized by antagonisms that bring to light both the contingency of the institutionalized frameworks of society within which everyday social practice takes place and the existence of other possible resolutions. In the "moment of antagonism," what happens is that "the undecidable nature of the alternatives and their resolution through power relations becomes fully visible."[26] It is this moment that constitutes "the political." The political itself is constitutive of social order—it is through the political that new social practices are instituted. Furthermore, the political, being a radical departure from sedimented

practices, "cannot appeal to anything in the social order that would operate as its ground: . . . [It] can only have its foundation in itself."[27]

SOVEREIGN POLITICS

In Western modernity what we call "politics" is a very specific notion, located within the conceptions of sovereignty: It entails a sovereign political
order and a sovereign, autonomous subject.[28] Foucault has argued that
"what we need . . . is a political philosophy that isn't erected around the
problem of sovereignty."[29] But the problem is not just that of sovereignty
or a sovereign politics. In his critique of Foucault, Barry Hindess points to
the need for a rethinking of "politics"; he notes that "it is not the problem
of sovereignty that *we* (another fictional community) need to free ourselves from, but also the problem of political community. In effect, this
means finding a way to think about politics in the absence of its defining,
constitutive fiction."[30]

Poststructuralist thought, in its move from "politics" to "the political,"
attempts to provide the tools for this rethinking. In Žižek's work on ideology, we have in particular an explicit focus on what Hindess calls for, that
is, "a more general investigation of the role of fictional communities in the
social and political thinking of western societies."

The approach of contemporary thinkers such as Foucault, Derrida,
Lacan, and Žižek is helpful here for two reasons. First, it does not see subjectivity and the social order as separable or separate in the first place. Hindess laments the way attention has been paid to the constitution of the
subject at the expense of understandings of community. But in a poststructuralist view the constitution of the subject entails and is inextricably linked
with the constitution of a particular social or symbolic order. Neither one
is prior to the other; indeed, notions of priority and separation are themselves bound up with particular modern conceptions of a sovereign subjectivity. Hindess accepts what he sees as Foucault's claim concerning "the
productivity of power in the formation of human attributes and capacities."[31] But is there a preexisting, nonsocial, human subject whose *attributes* and *capacities* remain as yet unformed? Is it not the very existence of
the subject as such that power relations constitute?[32] For Žižek, at least, as
we shall see, the formation of subjectivity implicates the social, whether or
not social existence is "organized" around principles such as sovereignty.

Second, for these thinkers there is not, as in some sense there appears
to be for Hindess, a "real" community to be found somewhere (behind, un-
derneath, beyond) the "fictional" communities that underpin political
thought. Žižek, for example, believes what we call "social reality" has the
status of a fiction but is no less real for all that. Moreover, there is nothing

behind it, concealed: The fiction conceals precisely the nothing or the lack at the heart of the social or symbolic order. Furthermore, it is not only the social, or "political community," that has the status of a fiction but also the subject. Through Žižek's work we are led directly to an exploration of the question of the political that does not see "the problem of political community" as one to be resolved, although the need for the fiction of political community and the fiction of the subject certainly must be examined. Žižek addresses these questions through a concern with ideology and subjectivity.

SUBJECTIVITY AS POLITICAL

The constitution of subjectivity and the social order are intricately bound up with each other, and sovereignty plays a pivotal role in both. But I want to discuss now more specifically how subjectivity is closely related to "the political" as I have distinguished it. I also want to relate that to ideology. Later chapters return to notions of subjectivity and—in a more muted form at first, in the guise of discussions of language and discourse—to ideology.

For Žižek, the political moment can be seen as the moment of subjectivity.[33] We have seen how the moment of the political is a period where a new social and political order is founded, a moment that by definition takes place without the authority of any existing political system or community. It institutes that which will henceforth count as "political community," and at the same time, as I discuss below, puts in place a narrative of its origins. At the time when the new order appears, however, its origins are completely without foundation.

The political moment, described elsewhere as a "nonfounded founding moment," is a turning point in history, a point "when 'something is happening'—open, undecidable."[34] It is a point at which the future is far from certain, a point at which anything can happen. Later, when a new social order has been established and the events that "led up to" it incorporated into history, these events may appear as part of some general historical development. At the time, however, "far from the exposition of an underlying necessity," what happens is that participants find themselves "confronted with responsibility, the burden of decision pressing upon [their] shoulders."[35] This situation is one in which people are forced to make decisions, to "act," in a manner for which they can find no guarantee in the social framework. That same framework is precisely missing, suspended, because it is in the process of reinvention. It is only by presuming the new social order, by "positing its presuppositions," that the new order is brought into being, retrospectively.

Žižek refers to the October Revolution as a situation of this type, where the impassioned debates among the various protagonists—V. I.

Lenin, Leon Trotsky, the Mensheviks—demonstrate that for them, at least, the outcome was certainly not as obvious as it appears when later described as arising out of a wider historical process.[36] Similar accounts of the radical contingency experienced at the time in contrast to a subsequent acceptance of the narration of events in a particular way can be found in relation to the events of 1989 in Europe. However much historians may deny it, it was not obvious at the time what the outcome would be.

There was a moment of openness, a political moment, in which the absence of one social order had not yet been succeeded by the presence of another, and at that time "acts" were precisely that: "acts" in the Lacanian sense—unsupported by any foundation of legitimacy in the social order. It is at this point that subjectivity arises. In Žižek's words: "This 'impossible' moment of openness constitutes the moment of *subjectivity:* 'subject' is a name for that unfathomable X called upon, suddenly made accountable, thrown into a position of responsibility, into the urgency of decision in such a moment of undecidability."[37]

Thus, moments of transition, where there is a sense of openness, of decision, are both moments of the political and moments in which subjectivity is called into play. They are also moments that constitute the social or symbolic order. Or rather, moments at which, through the presupposition of the existence of a new social system, such a system is brought into being. Not only is the new society founded, but it is produced as inevitable, authoritative, and legitimate: as if it has always already existed or been prophesied. The contingency of its origin is concealed.

 At that moment, once the foundational myth of the new social or symbolic order is (re)instated, the subject as such disappears, and with it the "political"—to be replaced by "politics." What is more, the interregnum, where there was a brief openness, is forgotten: de-scribed or un-written by the "writing" of the history of the new state. The act of the subject "succeeds by becoming invisible—by 'positivising' itself in a new symbolic network wherein it locates and explains itself as a result of historical process, thus reducing itself to a mere moment of the totality engendered by its own act."[38] This happens when events are "read" backward or retroactively: at that point it is easy to explain "objectively" why certain forces were effective and how particular tendencies "won." Indeed the Lacanian definition of "act" is just this: "a move that, so to speak, *defines its own conditions;* retroactively produces the grounds which justify it."[39]

This is where the notion of ideology as social fantasy, which I discuss in detail in Chapter 6, comes in. Once the new symbolic order is in place, the contingencies that gave rise to it are obliterated—they disappear—and a new version of social reality is established. The role of ideology here is to conceal the illegitimate, unfounded nature of what we call social reality, what Žižek calls "social fantasy." Ideology supports the principle of legitimacy upon which the new state is "founded" and conceals its "impossibility." It does this in part by defining "politics" as a subsystem of the social order and obliterating "the political"—its unfounded founding moment: "'Politics' as 'subsystem,' as a separate sphere of society, represents *within* society its own forgotten foundation, its genesis in a violent abyssal act—it represents, within the social space, what must *fall out* if this space is to constitute itself."[40] Or as Žižek expresses it more provocatively, "Politics as subsystem is a metaphor of the political subject, of the Political as subject."[41]

In other words, it is "politics," viewed as one of the subsystems of all the systems that go to make up the social order, that enables us to escape or forget the lack of "the political" and the absence of the possibility of any political action. We are confined by this process to activity within the boundaries set by existing social and international orders, and our criticism is restricted to the technical arrangements that make up the "politics" within which we exist as "subjects" of the state. The political subject and the international subject, too, are safely caged and their teeth pulled.

DEPOLITICIZATION AND TECHNOLOGIZATION

It is precisely the operation through which the political subject is tamed that I refer to as "depoliticization" and technologization. As I mentioned above, I use the two terms more or less interchangeably, though I prefer the latter since it gives a view of a more explicit, active process rather than a mere absence. I say a little about how I understand technologization and then set out how the thinkers I analyze contribute to this understanding.

In modern Western societies, "politics" is limited to the calculable, the instrumental: "Politics in the age of technology means the total domination of rational calculability and planning, the triumph of instrumental reason."[42] Michael Dillon's Heideggerean reading sees technologization as cutting off human being from its sense of self, from all that it might mean to be human: "Technology, one might therefore say, makes human being flat-footed in respect of its ethical comportment towards itself as the uncanny—both native and stranger to itself—being with others in the face of the Otherness that it is."[43] International politics is a specific site where technologization occurs. International relations as a discipline "dissipates the concern with the political and substitutes, instead, a fascination with the manifold globalised and globalising technologies of order that have emerged to administer human being."[44] An understanding of "the political" is not taught or researched but rather replaced by a study of "the technology of calculative order."[45]

Processes of technologization or depoliticization can be seen in international politics itself, as well as in the discipline that studies it. One example of this is found in responses to famines, humanitarian crises, or complex political emergencies.[46] Agencies and governments outside the crisis area do not take account of the political processes that are under way, of which the crisis is a symptom. Instead, they rely on interventions derived from an abstract, technical analysis of the situation, one that looks for "causes," not political reasons or motivations.

In the case of a "famine," they analyze the situation in terms of crop production, food availability, and the nutritional status of the population. Systems are put in place that give early warnings of impending famines based on such factors, occasionally including "social" action such as movement of peoples in search of food or employment. This analysis is unhelpful for two reasons. First, it means that assistance to deprived populations can take place only when the criteria for recognizing a "famine" have been satisfied: generally, when starvation, disease, or displacement has led to mass starvation—already too late for assistance to be of any use. Second, it means that the assistance that is provided is given in a manner that often plays into the hands of the political opponents of the famine victims. Food aid can be used to feed armies as well as the starving; it can provide an economy of "permanent emergency"[47] from which certain sectors of the population will benefit at the expense of others' suffering. Food aid can also serve the political ends of the donors, whether governments or agencies. David Keen has analyzed these processes at work in the Sudan famines of the 1980s.[48] Methods of administration of food aid programs even in peacetime involve a technologization and depoliticization. Food-for-work programs in Eritrea in the 1990s provide examples of disciplinary processes and technologization in practice: I have discussed these in detail elsewhere.[49]

It is now generally recognized that aid and famine relief carry the risk of worsening the situation, but this does not prevent further attempts at "technologizing" what have come to be called "complex emergencies."[50] Once it is seen that famines often involve conflict, analysis turns to the features of conflict rather than the nutritional status of famine victims, and this in turn produces various techniques of conflict analysis and resolution.[51] What is still not widely understood is that processes of emergency in crises signaled by famines, conflicts, and wars are just that: processes of the emergence of new political structures.[52] It is precisely in such instances that we find "the political." The common "methods" of response do not grasp this and instead seek to impose a technology of either nutritional analysis, conflict control, or "doing no harm."[53] In an important sense, though, as with all attempts at technologization, what is being done *is,* after all, intensely "political." It involves the suppression of the new forms of political order whose emergence the emergency announces.

A second example in the field of international politics is the process of securitization.[54] Securitization, or claiming that something is an issue of national security, removes it from one arena within which it is debated contested in a certain way and takes it to another, where the priorities are different. Once something has been "securitized," this changes the terms of the debate. Certain questions can no longer be asked. In the security studies literature, securitization is seen as a further step beyond what is called there "politicization." Barry Buzan, Ole Waever, and Jaap de Wilde explain how they see "securitization":

> "Security" is the move that takes politics beyond the established rules of the game and frames the issue either as a special kind of politics or as above politics. Securitization can thus be seen as a more extreme version of politicization. In theory any public issue can be located on the spectrum ranging from nonpoliticized (meaning the state does not deal with it and it is not in any other way made an issue of public debate and decision) through politicized (meaning the issue is part of public policy, requiring government decision and resource allocations or, more rarely, some other form of communal governance) to securitized (meaning the issue is presented as an existential threat, requiring emergency measures and justifying actions outside the normal bounds of political procedure).[55]

Buzan, Waever, and de Wilde's use of "politicized" is quite distinct from what mine would be.[56] What they call "politicization" I would call "depoliticization": When an issue becomes, as they say, "part of public policy, requiring government decision and resource allocations," it becomes for me part of "politics" and hence, as I have argued above, "depoliticized." I would agree that securitization is a further step in the same direction, but for me that direction is one of depoliticization. When issues are "securitized," they are even more firmly constrained within the already accepted criteria of a specific social form. And that constraint is even more firmly denied. The state as a form of society has defined itself in large part around what it will consider as "security threat" and what mechanisms it will adopt for dealing with it. Issues of "security" are more removed from public debate and decision than issues of "politics"; in most cases these issues are secret, and even the existence of such matters is concealed. Decisions about them are taken in technical terms, following the advice of experts in military affairs or defense. Securitization is technologization par excellence.

In Chapters 3–6 I examine the work of Foucault, Derrida, Lacan, and Žižek. These writers provide us with the tools for a reassessment of the possibility of the political, and they examine processes of depoliticization and technologization. Foucault's work centers on three "axes of genealogy": the truth axis, where subjects of knowledge are produced in the "sciences"; the power axis, where patterns of normalization or discipline are produced through subjects' acting on others in "dividing practices"; and the ethics axis. Two aspects of technologization or depoliticization appear here. The first, from the truth axis, is in Foucault's notion of "régimes of truth" and what he sees as the role of science and technology in the modern *episteme*. For Foucault, "truth" is linked in a circular relation with power: Power and knowledge are mutually constitutive. This means that "the political question . . . is truth itself," and how something gets to count as true is a political process.[57] When the production of truth is claimed to be a search for objective "knowledge," it is depoliticized. In our society the production of truth is "centred on the form of scientific discourse and the institutions which produce it."[58] The politics of truth in Western capitalist societies has led to the hegemony of "scientific" forms of truth; scientific discourse is the dominant form of political practice.

The second aspect of technologization, on the power axis, comes from the notion of dividing practices. In his disciplinary model, Foucault argues that in addition to punishment, prison has a technodisciplinary aspect that operates through surveillance, isolation, work programs, and the offer of remission in exchange for compliance. This is a depoliticizing and controlling process, one that produces a distinct "subject" (the delinquent) and the techniques of producing "knowledge" about that subject (the discipline of criminology). It is a search for order, discipline, and regulation. The failure of prisons in their (apparent) aim of rehabilitation is in actuality a success. This success rests in the way that, by criminalizing, they depoliticize: The political force of certain acts—forms of protest or dissent, for example—is removed. A way to repoliticize, a "political act," would be to interrupt discourse, to challenge what have, through discursive practices, been constituted as normal, natural, and accepted ways of carrying on.

Derrida's work echoes this concern for dividing practices and how power, force, or violence is implicated (but concealed). Derrida argues that Western metaphysics—the metaphysics of presence or logocentrism—relies on a process of differentiating through hierarchical binaries or opposites. He shows that in pairs of opposites—written/spoken, presence/absence, man/woman, constative/performative, for example—the first term is always marked by traces of the second, which is both "deferred" and differentiated. The second is the "constitutive outside" of the first—the "outside" that is also inside, necessary to the constitution of the "essence." The stability of this process is not assured. It contains within itself the possibility of deconstruction.

These hierarchical oppositions, an inherent part of logocentrism, have political implications. They embody the force or violence of a "founding moment." Deconstruction consists in a double gesture, both a reversal of the hierarchy and a displacement. Although a simple inversion does not challenge the *form* of the opposition, such a move may be necessary for strategic reasons. But the results of any deconstructive move are "incalculable." The notion of the relation of force or violence to *logos* returns in Derrida's discussion of the force of law and the impossibility of justice;

this also leads to the elaboration of a distinction between a calculable "technology" and an incalculable ethics or politics.

Law always implies a force, both that involved in the notion of enforcement and that captured in its founding moment. The founding moment is the moment of decisioning, the moment that both produces and reproduces the law. It is, as we have discussed above, the moment of "the political." Central to Derrida's argument here is the notion of following a rule. The concept of justice requires the concept of following the law or rule as well as the concept of acting in a "free" and responsible way. Following the law (if that were possible) would not be "just"; it would merely involve a calculable process. But a decision cannot anyway just follow the law: Each case in which a decision is made is different, specific, and particular; there is always a need for interpretation, which itself, once it has been done, has "produced" the law. The law is not guaranteed in advance. It is not known afterward, either, whether the decision was a "just" act or not. Indeed, Derrida argues, justice is impossible. This is related to the notion of the undecidable, the "essential ghost" in every decision that deconstructs it from within. The "ordeal of the undecidable"[59] must be gone through, but it is a terrifying moment of suspense. The foundational moment, however, remains hidden: Presence (and certainty) is instituted through a (political) moment of decision, one that involves force and an unavoidable violence. The ethicopolitical process of decisioning involves finding possible (impossible) answers; without the decision we would merely be following a program, applying a technology.

The notion of a foundational moment that is necessary to constitute presence but which must remain unacknowledged links Derrida's work to conceptualizations of the ideological that we see in Žižek's Lacanian approach, where the ideological is implicated in the very existence of (what we call) social reality. What is at stake for Žižek is the role of ideology in concealing the inherently antagonistic nature of all attempts at "society"; all (impossible) attempts to constitute a meaningful social reality hide the traumatic "real." The role of the master signifier in Žižek's account echoes the ghostliness of undecidability in Derrida's. For Žižek, the political act, the critique of ideology, is to "occupy the place of the lack" or master signifier, drawing attention to its constructed and political force, making it impossible for it to be "naturalized" or fully stabilized. The argument would be that we should persist in the "impossible" position, the empty place, or undecidable split. This is the place of the specter or ghost, that which escapes (at the moment of decision). Persisting in this position means drawing attention to how any social system is inherently antagonistic (and hence "political," as Laclau sees it).

Žižek sees the role of the master signifier as crucial in giving an account of the authoritarian form of discourse and how it captures our desire. The constitution of the subject and the constitution of the social or symbolic

order take place simultaneously, through the intervention of the master signifier, which distorts the symbolic field at the same time as establishing it
(temporarily). The master signifier stands for and conceals the lack, the
void, around which the symbolic order is constituted; the subject is also
constituted around a primordial lack, and interpellation into the symbolic
order enables the subject to "forget" the traumatic "lack" in an acceptance
of the symbolic. This is the function of the ideological—to enable social
reality as an escape from the real. The social order ("politics") effaces the
traces of its own impossibility. It is naturalized, depoliticized.

CONCLUSION

What makes the process of technologization work? It works through and
by means of—by producing—a particular linear notion of time, a view of
knowledge as separable from the political (or power), a subject that pre-
exists politics, and a notion of the real as separable from thought about it.
In concluding this discussion of politics, subjectivity, and depoliticization,
I want to summarize how poststructuralist, deconstructivist, and psychoanalytic thought challenges these notions. In doing this, of course, such
thinking provides the tools for an understanding of depoliticization and an
examination of the possibility of a repoliticization, to which I return in the
last chapter of this book.

The first challenge is to the linear notion of time. Derrida draws our
attention to how the "metaphysics of presence," a belief in the obviousness
and presence of the here and now, the present time, is specific to logocentrism, to modernity's understanding of itself.[60] He demonstrates how unstable and difficult this notion of the present and presence is. In Foucault
we find a parallel insistence on the notion of a "history of the present." We
cannot look on the past with anything other than the eyes of the present—
so all we are attempting in a sense is an account *viewed with our eyes.*
Hence the words "archaeology" and "genealogy," to indicate a relation between Foucault's account and his subject matter that is not one of history.
It is not a question of discovering "history" but of producing "a genealogy."[61] Both Derrida and Žižek, but perhaps particularly Žižek, emphasize
how fickle the idea of a linear form of time is. The Derridean notion of *différance,* which he proposes to replace the logocentric "metaphysics of
presence," incorporates the ideas both of difference and deferral.[62] It has
a time dimension built in. In Žižek's Lacanian approach, too, the constitution of the subject is a process that cannot be envisaged other than by
seeing time as in a sense going backward. Things become what they already were only retrospectively, through discursive or ideological
processes. Lacan's *point de capiton* is the "quilting point" at which the

sliding of signifiers is arrested by a backward stitch to "produce" the object as it already was.[63] These views of time render notions of cause and effect, essence and change untenable.

The notion of language as a neutral medium of communication is disputed, as is any possibility of objective "truth" or knowledge. Foucault made the close relationship between power and knowledge clear in his discussion of "power/knowledge." Truth is produced through discourse: "'Truth' is linked in a circular relation with systems of power which produce and sustain it, and to effects of power which it induces and which extend it."[64] In this régime of truth, truth and meaning are produced discursively and are intimately bound up with the political, as the term "régime" suggests: "Each society has its régime of truth, its 'general politics' of truth."[65] Derrida makes the same link. He sees binary opposites as already hierarchical and containing violence. The performative is in itself an act of power linked with the social institution that supports the enunciation.[66] In Žižek, too, we find the notion of the act of naming, or interpellation, as a violent act that produces the subject (or the object) as such.[67] These notions have implications for our understanding of the political, the drawing of limits and frontiers, and processes of exclusion.

Problematized notions of time throw into question the possibility of "essence" and of any preexisting subject or object. In Foucault the subject and the social are constituted through processes of exclusion, separating the mad from the sane or the criminal from the others. In Derrida this becomes the notion of the constitutive outside, the supplement that is at one and the same time both necessary (for the subject to exist at all) and too much.[68] In Žižek's Lacanian analysis, it becomes the notion of the surplus and the lack. Derrida and Žižek alike see closure as impossible, though the drive to, or desire for, closure or the totality produces the surplus. This supplement/surplus has an ambiguous relationship to the things it constitutes: It is both internal and external to them. This conceptualization leads to a particular notion of space as folded in upon itself, similar to the curved space of Einsteinian physics.[69] We have what at first sight seems to be a process of drawing boundaries but turns out to enclose or produce that which it tries to exclude.

Finally, the fourth notion that Foucault, Derrida, and Žižek problematize is the notion of reality or the real. They question whether there is such a realm, in the sense of one that can be distinguished from some other realm, the realm of "ideas," the discursive, texts, or illusion. They challenge notions of the distinction itself, between the discursive and the nondiscursive (Foucault), the text and *hors-texte* (Derrida), and reality and illusion (Žižek).[70] For Žižek, in his reading of Lacan, what we call "social reality"— the symbolic order—is precisely that which is produced by the exclusion of "the real"—that which cannot be symbolized. What is important is not the distinction between reality and "ideas," between a world "out there" and our ideas about it, but how effects of truth (for Foucault) or effects of reality (for Žižek) are produced. According to Žižek, ideology and processes of repression or forgetting produce the social by excluding the real.[71]

I have outlined the challenges that poststructuralist, deconstructivist, and psychoanalytic thought poses to questions of time, essence, and language. The remaining chapters elaborate these points in more detail as they explore new notions of the subject and ideology. It is in part through these challenges that this strand of contemporary thought offers a route to repoliticization, and the final chapter returns to discuss this possibility. Perhaps the most powerful (and the most unyielding) of the assumptions on which technologization is founded is that of the preexisting subject. Subsequent chapters pursue this question and analyze the notion of subjectivity as a basis for examining "the political." I show how language, as the symbolic or social order, is implicated in subjectivity. In Chapter 2 I begin by considering how Cartesian assumptions about the subject have been challenged and the subject decentered.

NOTES

1. See, for example, Ernesto Laclau, "Introduction," and Ernesto Laclau and Lilian Zac, "Minding the Gap: The Subject of Politics," in *The Making of Political Identities*, ed. Ernesto Laclau (London: Verso, 1994), 1–8, 11–39; Claude Lefort, *Democracy and Political Theory*, trans. David Macey (Cambridge: Polity, 1988); Philippe Lacoue-Labarthe, *Heidegger, Art and Politics: The Fiction of the Political* (Oxford: Blackwell, 1990).

2. Michael Dillon, *Politics of Security: Towards a Political Philosophy of Continental Thought*, trans. Chris Turner (London: Routledge, 1996), 52–56.

3. For a discussion of some of the debates, see Simon Critchley, *The Ethics of Deconstruction: Derrida and Levinas* (Oxford: Blackwell, 1992), 200–219.

4. Max Weber, *The Theory of Social and Economic Organization,* trans. A. M. Henderson and Talcott Parsons (New York: Free Press, 1947).

5. Žižek's work is discussed in Chapters 5 and 6. For these points, see, for example, Slavoj Žižek, *For They Know Not What They Do: Enjoyment as a Political Factor* (London: Verso, 1991).

6. James Donald and Stuart Hall, *Politics and Ideology* (Milton Keynes, UK: Open University Press, 1986), xiv.

7. Cynthia Enloe, "Conclusion: The Personal Is International," in *Bananas, Beaches and Bases: Making Feminist Sense of International Politics* (Berkeley: University of California Press, 1990), 195–201.

8. Fred Dallmayr, *The Other Heidegger* (Ithaca, NY: Cornell University Press, 1993), quoted in Dillon, *Politics of Security,* 213.

9. Lefort, *Democracy and Political Theory* 11; quoted in Dillon, *Politics of Security,* 213.

10. Ibid.

11. Claude Lefort, *The Political Forms of Modern Society,* trans. John B. Thompson (Cambridge: Polity, 1986), 282 (my emphasis).

12. Ibid., 282.

13. Ibid., 284.

14. Žižek, *For They Know Not What They Do,* 193–195. The distinction between "the political" and "politics" parallels that between *le politique* and *la politique,* made by Philippe Lacoue-Labarthe and Jean-Luc Nancy. We could say that *le politique* corresponds to "the political" as I have discussed it here and *la politique* to "politics": "*Le politique* refers to the essence of the political . . . whereas *la politique* refers to the facticity, or empirical event of politics"; Critchley, *Ethics of Deconstruction,* 201. For a discussion of Lacoue-Labarthe and Nancy's work, see ibid., 200–219. Critchley refers to discussions in Nancy Fraser, "The French Derrideans: Politicising Deconstruction or Deconstructing the Political?" *New German Critique,* 33 (1984): 127–154; and David Ingram, "The Retreat of the Political in the Modern Age: Jean-Luc Nancy on Totalitarianism and Community," *Research on Phenomenology,* 18 (1988): 93–124. On a similar topic, the works of Alain Badiou, for example, *Peut-on penser la politique?* (Paris: Le Seuil, 1985) and *L'Être et l'événement* (Paris: Le Seuil, 1988), are interesting.

15. H. H. Gerth and C. Wright Mills, eds. and trans., *From Max Weber: Essays in Sociology* (London: Routledge, 1948), 228. Weber argues that the success of bureaucracy means that coups d'état are substituted for revolutions: "such a [bureaucratic] machine makes 'revolution,' in the sense of the forceful creation of entirely new formations of authority, technically more and more impossible" (ibid., 230).

16. Max Weber, "Politics as a Vocation," in ibid., 77.

17. Ibid., 78.

18. Ibid., 77–128.

19. Ibid., 127.

20. Weber, *Theory of Social and Economic Organization,* 363–364.

21. See, for example, Enloe, *Bananas, Beaches and Bases*; Jean Bethke Elshtain, *Public Man, Private Woman: Women in Social and Political Thought,* 2nd ed. (Princeton, NJ: Princeton University Press, 1993).

22. Jacques Derrida, "Force of Law: The 'Mystical Foundation of Authority,'" in *Deconstruction and the Possibility of Justice,* ed. David Gray Carlson, Drucilla Cornell, and Michel Rosenfeld (New York: Routledge, 1992), 3–67.

23. Jacques Derrida, *The Other Heading: Reflections on Today's Europe,* trans. Pascale-Anne Brault and Michael B. Naas (Bloomington: Indiana University Press, 1992), 44.

24. Ernesto Laclau, *New Reflections on the Revolution of Our Time* (London: Verso, 1990), 35.

25. Ibid., 2.

26. Ibid., 35.

27. Ibid., 4.

28. Jenny Edkins and Véronique Pin-Fat, "The Subject of the Political," in *Sovereignty and Subjectivity,* ed. Jenny Edkins, Nalini Persram, and Véronique Pin-Fat (Boulder, CO: Lynne Rienner, 1999), 1–18.

29. Michel Foucault, *Power/Knowledge: Selected Interviews and Other Writings, 1972–1977,* ed. Colin Gordon, trans. Colin Gordon, Leo Marshall, John Mepham, and Kate Soper (Brighton, UK: Harvester, 1980), 121.

30. Barry Hindess, *Discourses of Power: From Hobbes to Foucault* (Oxford: Blackwell, 1996), 158.

31. Ibid., 155–156.

32. Foucault himself makes this clear when he claims that "the individual is not a pregiven entity which is seized on by the exercise of power. The individual, *with* his identity and characteristics, is the product of a relation of power exercised

over bodies, multiplicities, desires, forces." Foucault, *Power/Knowledge,* 73–74 (my emphasis).

33. Žižek, *For They Know Not What They Do,* 189.

34. Ibid., 188–189.

35. Ibid., 189.

36. Ibid.

37. Ibid.

38. Ibid., 191.

39. Ibid., 192.

40. Ibid., 194.

41. Ibid.

42. Critchley, *Ethics of Deconstruction,* 204.

43. Dillon, *Politics of Security,* 52. This evokes Julia Kristeva's work on the uncanny in *Strangers to Ourselves,* trans. Leon S. Roudiez (New York: Columbia University Press, 1991), 182–192.

44. Dillon, *Politics of Security,* 52.

45. Ibid., 53.

46. I have discussed in more detail elsewhere how processes of technologization are to be found not only in practices of famine relief but also in the theoretical approaches that underpin them. See Jenny Edkins, "Legality with a Vengeance: Famines and Humanitarian Relief in 'Complex Emergencies,'" *Millennium,* 25, 3 (1996): 547–575.

47. This is Mark Duffield's phrase; see in particular Mark Duffield, "NGOs, Disaster Relief and Asset Transfer in the Horn: Political Survival in a Permanent Emergency," *Development and Change,* 24, 1 (1993): 131–157.

48. David Keen, *The Benefits of Famine: A Political Economy of Famine and Relief in Southwestern Sudan, 1983–1989* (Princeton, NJ: Princeton University Press, 1994).

49. Jenny Edkins, *Famines and Modernity: Pictures of Hunger, Concepts of Famine, Practices of Aid* (Minneapolis: University of Minnesota Press, forthcoming).

50. Ironically, these were at one time called "complex *political* emergencies" by those who wished to emphasize the political element in famines. This failed to prevent their retechnologization: We now have an emerging "technology" of complex emergencies.

51. David Keen and Ken Wilson, "Engaging with Violence: A Reassessment of Relief in Wartime," in *War and Hunger: Rethinking International Responses to Complex Emergencies,* ed. Joanna Macrae and Anthony Zwi (London: Zed Books, 1994), 209–221.

52. Dillon has called this "the emergence of new political complexes." See, for example, the discussion in the workshop on the politics of emergency reported in Jenny Edkins, ed., "The Politics of Emergency," *Manchester Papers in Politics,* 2, 1997.

53. For a discussion that can arguably be seen as the latest move of this retechnologization, see Mary B. Anderson, *Do No Harm: How Aid Can Support Peace—or War* (Boulder, CO: Lynne Rienner, 1999). Anderson sets out criteria for ensuring that interventions bring benefits only to the victims of crisis; unfortunately, this still assumes that general rules and techniques can be derived that are applicable to "political" situations.

54. I discuss this in more detail in Jenny Edkins, "International Security," in *Post-Structuralism and Politics: An Introduction,* ed. Alan Finlayson and Jeremy Valentine (Edinburgh: Edinburgh University Press, forthcoming).

55. Barry Buzan, Ole Waever, and Jaap de Wilde, *Security: A New Framework for Analysis* (Boulder, CO: Lynne Rienner, 1998), 23–24. See also Ole Waever, "Securitization and Desecuritization," in *On Security,* ed. Ronnie D. Lipschutz (New York: Columbia University Press, 1995), 46–86.

56. In the discussion above, I have not had recourse to a term for "politicization" for the precise reason that I do not regard an originary "politicization" as necessary (though a *re*politicization of course may well be). Buzan, Waever, and de Wilde do somewhat contradict this reading later when they argue that "politicization means to make an issue *appear to be* open, a matter of choice, something that is decided upon and that therefore entails responsibility, in contrast to issues that either could not be different (laws of nature) or should not be put under political control (e.g., a free economy, the private sphere, and matters for expert decision)"; ibid., 29 (my emphasis). However, my argument would be that things are "open" until a political decision depoliticizes them and makes them *appear* issues not of responsibility but of expertise or technology.

57. Foucault, *Power/Knowledge,* 133.

58. Ibid., 131.

59. Derrida, "Force of Law," 24–25.

60. See, for example, Jacques Derrida, *Positions,* trans. Alan Bass (London: Athlone Press, 1987).

61. Michel Foucault, "Nietzsche, Genealogy, History," in *Language, Counter-memory, Practice: Selected Essays and Interviews,* ed. Donald F. Bouchard, trans. Donald F. Bouchard and Sherry Smith (Ithaca, NY: Cornell University Press, 1977), 139–164.

62. See, for example, Jacques Derrida, *Writing and Difference,* trans. Alan Bass (London: Routledge, 1978).

63. Jacques Lacan, *Écrits: A Selection,* trans. Alan Sheridan (London: Routledge, 1980).

64. Foucault, *Power/Knowledge,* 133.

65. Ibid., 131.

66. Jacques Derrida, "Signature Event Context," in *Limited Inc,* ed. Jacques Derrida, trans. Samuel Weber and Jeffrey Mehlman (Evanston, IL: Northwestern University Press, 1988), 1–23.

67. Slavoj Žižek, *The Sublime Object of Ideology* (London: Verso, 1989).

68. The notion of the constitutive outside comes from Henry Staten's reading of Derrida, as I discuss in Chapter 4. See Henry Staten, *Wittgenstein and Derrida* (Oxford: Blackwell, 1984). See, further, Jacques Derrida, *Of Grammatology,* trans. Gayatri Chakravorty Spivak (Baltimore, MD: Johns Hopkins University Press, 1976), 140–167.

69. Slavoj Žižek, *Looking Awry: An Introduction to Jacques Lacan Through Popular Culture* (Cambridge: MIT Press, 1991), 135–136.

70. Michel Foucault, *The Archaeology of Knowledge,* trans. A. M. Sheridan Smith (London: Routledge, 1989); Derrida, *Writing and Difference;* Žižek, *For They Know Not What They Do.*

71. In Lacanian theory, "the real" is sometimes written with an uppercase "R" and sometimes not. Here I will use the lowercase unless I am quoting from another source. The distinction between "the real" (or "the Real") and "reality" is discussed further in Chapter 6. See also Bruce Fink, *The Lacanian Subject: Between Language and Jouissance* (Princeton, NJ: Princeton University Press, 1995), 24–25.

2

Decentering the Subject

The Cartesian subject—the conscious, fully aware, rational subject—plays a crucial role in the epistemology of the Enlightenment. Its articulation is based on the distinction between doubt and certainty, a distinction closely related to that between truth and illusion found in the discussion of certain views of ideology. Rejecting as a foundation for philosophy everything of which there could be any doubt, Descartes tells us:

> I became aware that, while I decided thus to think that everything was false, it followed necessarily that I who thought thus must be something: and observing that this truth: *I think, therefore I am,* was so certain and so evident that all the most extravagant suppositions of the sceptics were not capable of shaking it, I judged that I could accept it without scruple. . . . I thereby concluded that I was a substance, of which the whole essence or nature consists in thinking, and which, in order to exist, needs no place and depends on no material thing; so that this "I", that is to say, the mind, by which I am what I am, is entirely distinct from the body, and even that it is easier to know than the body.[1]

The Enlightenment subject was a unified individual with a center, an inner core that was there at birth and developed as the individual grew, while remaining essentially the same. This core of the self was the source of the subject's identity.

Contemporary philosophy has followed the natural sciences in shattering this notion, which was linked with a cosmology that put "man" at the center of the universe, and has decentered the subject itself. Stuart Hall, sees two stages in this process: first the move from the Enlightenment subject to the sociological subject, then the move to the postmodern subject. He describes the move to the sociological subject as one that "reflected the growing complexity of the modern world and the awareness that this inner core of the subject was not autonomous and self-sufficient, but was formed in relation to 'significant others,' who mediated to the subject the values, meanings and symbols—the culture—of the worlds he/she inhabited."[2] This was an interactive conception of identity and the self. The identity of the subject was formed (or constructed) in the interaction between self and society. For the socially constructed subject, identity bridges the gap between inside and outside. "The subject still has an inner core or essence . . . but this is formed and modified in a continuous dialogue with the cultural worlds 'outside' and the identities which they offer."[3] Identity sutures the subject into the structure, stabilizing both. The notion of the sociological subject acknowledges processes of socialization and the influence of different historical and geographical cultures and subcultures. Crucially, however, the distinction between the individual *and* society still holds, and resolving problems of how the two relate to each other assumes a central significance.

The postmodern subject, by contrast, has no fixed, essential, or permanent identity. Subjectivity is formed and transformed in a continuous process that takes place in relation to the ways we are represented or addressed and alongside the production or reproduction of the social. Hall argues that five major theoretical moves have produced this further decentering of the Cartesian subject. These are found in the work of Karl Marx, Sigmund Freud, Ferdinand de Saussure, Foucault, and the feminists.[4] The subject is decentered, first, by the proposition that language is not a tool to express ideas about reality; rather, the speaking subject is always already embedded in a preexisting language structure. Naming produces things rather than attaching labels to "objects" that are already there, and language is social and eludes individual or collective will. Saussure's disruption of the picture of language as a neutral tool is accompanied by Freud's questioning of the rational, transparent character of thought itself. For Freud, consciousness is not primary but only an aspect of the unconscious. Freud's analysis leads to an account of the process of "dream work," the secret of the dream, which lies in its form, not its content, in terms of overdetermination, condensation, displacement, and representation. Feminist decenterings challenge the notion of the subject as unsexed, gender neutral, and disembodied. Feminism reveals the supposedly universal Cartesian subject as a white Protestant male heterosexual and explores the implications of different notions of the body. It points out how in our setting subjects are produced as gendered, and how at the same time a social system that is built on gender hierarchies is reproduced. The final decentering, in the work of Marx, extends the "always already" beyond language, to the social structure. Preexisting, historic, social conditions frame action, which anyway determines consciousness rather than being determined by it. In other words, consciousness, which Freud showed to be secondary, is anyhow not what it appears. This chapter examines these decenterings and provides the setting for the discussions in the following chapters on the work of Foucault, Derrida, and Žižek, which draw on many of the concepts introduced here.

LANGUAGE GAMES

The Cartesian subject is a subject founded on thought. Saussure's linguistics challenges and decenters this subject by questioning the possibility of regarding ideas or thoughts as either individual or transparent in the way that Descartes takes for granted. Saussure, by contrast, regards ideas as social, mutable, and changing. Saussure's work on language was a radical break with previous linguistics, which had concentrated in the main on tracing the evolution over time of linguistic patterns, called diachrony. Saussure's interest is in examining the state of language as a system at a particular point in time, or synchronic linguistics. It is this always already existing system that the speaking, thinking subject confronts. Saussure makes a number of distinctions, the first between language (*langue*) and human speech (*langage*) and the second between *langue* and *parole*. He sees *parole* as the more or less individual act of the speaker "speaking"; *langue,* in contrast, is not a function of the speaker but "the social side of speech, outside the individual who can never create or modify it by himself; it exists only by virtue of a sort of contract signed by the members of a community."[5] This is what he concentrates on exploring—language as a system of signs that express ideas. It was a new science, semiology, "a science that studies the life of signs within society."[6] For Saussure, a distinctive characteristic of the sign is the way it eludes the individual or social will.

Saussure's approach to language also challenged the accepted view of the process of naming. This view assumed that ready-made "ideas" existed before the process began: Naming was then a simple linking of name and object. According to Saussure, the linguistic sign (the sign) unites not a thing and a name but a concept (the signified) and a sound image (the signifier), both of which are psychological. The process has two characteristics. The first is the arbitrary nature of the sign. The bond between the signifier and signified is arbitrary, and hence the whole (the linguistic sign) is arbitrary, too (which of course does *not* mean that an individual can change it). The second characteristic is the linear nature of the signifier. The signifier, being auditory, is unfolded in time. Signifiers form a chain.

A crucial point here is that the signifier is not mutable: "The signifier, though to all appearances freely chosen with respect to the idea that it represents, is fixed, not free, with respect to the linguistic community that uses it. The masses have no voice in the matter, and the signifier chosen by language could be replaced by no other."[7] This is largely because of the always already, pregiven nature of language as a system: "No matter what period we choose or how far back we go, language always appears as a heritage of the preceding period."[8] Any speaker is confronted with a specific linguistic state. The sign, however, is at the same time mutable. Change takes place when there is a shift in the relationship between the signifier and the signified, and in fact language is described as being radically powerless to defend itself against the forces of change. This is seen as a consequence of the arbitrariness of the sign. "Language is a system whose parts can and must all be considered in their synchronic solidarity. . . . Since changes never affect the system as a whole but rather one or another of its elements, they can be studied only outside the system."[9] Changes to one element reverberate through the whole system.

Linguistic terms have "values" that owe their existence solely to usage within the system that is generally accepted by the community: "Language is a system of interdependent terms in which the value of each term results solely from the simultaneous presence of the others."[10] To establish a value, two things are necessary: dissimilar things, for which the thing of value can be exchanged (in language this is signification, where a word is exchanged for an idea), and similar things, with which the thing can be compared (in language this is other words). The value of a term is determined by its environment. Thus there is no exact correspondence of values between languages. If words stood for preexisting concepts, there would be.

It is worth emphasizing these two points to summarize the radical nature of Saussure's approach: (1) Words are part of a language *system:* "Within the same language all words used to express related concepts limit each other reciprocally. . . . Words are enriched through contact with others."[11] (2) Words do not stand for *preexisting* concepts (there are no exact equivalences in different languages): "In language there are only differences. . . . Language has neither ideas nor sounds that existed before the linguistic system, but only conceptual and phonic differences that have issued from the system."[12] This holds when the signifier and the signified are considered separately; when they are considered as a totality, as sign, what the linguistic system contains is a system of values. Signs are *positive* terms: "When we compare signs—positive terms—with each other, we can no longer speak of *difference.*"[13] Two signs, each with a signifier and a signified, are not different but *distinct.* Between them there is only opposition.

A language state is based on relations, and Saussure distinguishes two forms: syntagms and associations. Syntagms arise because of the linearity of relations in speech: The speaker cannot say two things at once, so relations are with what was said before and what follows. But associations take place outside discourse, through memory. Associations may be of meaning or form or a combination of both. In discourse (which for Saussure means "in speaking") both types of relations operate together. The speaker's choice of syntagm will be influenced by the associations it evokes. A particular sign is not "chosen" because it signifies what the speaker wants to express. "In reality the idea evokes not a form but a whole latent system that makes possible the oppositions necessary for the formation of the sign. By itself the sign would have no signification."[14] What Saussure shows, according to Françoise Gadet, is that the subject is not in charge of language, and "in studying language as an abstract object—a system whose mechanisms are external both to the individual and physical reality—Saussurian theory contributed to the deconstruction of the free and conscious psychological subject dominant in philosophical thought."[15]

But the potential of Saussure's work was not followed up immediately. It led to structuralism, the synchronic analysis of a system and its structural relations. But its more radical potential, based on its view of the active function of the signifier in creating and determining the signified, was not pursued.[16] As Gadet argues, the followers of Saussure can be split into two camps: structuralists and poststructuralists. In the first camp would be Roland Barthes and Claude Lévi-Strauss, for whom "the transfer of essentially unreconstructed concepts from linguistics results in the preservation of the idea of a human nature as a specific object and an explanatory principle." In the second camp, Lacan, Derrida, Foucault, and Louis Althusser would, in contrast, reject this notion of the subject; "their so-called 'antihumanism' amounts to the abandonment of transcendental subjectification: the fact that language is always-already there defines the subject as position, never as substance."[17]

In his early works, Barthes is undoubtedly a structuralist, drawing certain notions from Saussure while at the same time trying to retain a positivist epistemology. He breaks languages into elements to recombine these within a system and distinguishes different levels of movement from reality as "denotative" and "connotative" languages and "metalanguages." In *Mythologies* he takes as his starting point the insight of Saussure into the arbitrariness of the sign and traces examples of "ideological processes" by which bourgeois signs pass themselves off as natural signs.[18] As Terry Eagleton explains it, "Signs which pass themselves off as natural, which offer themselves as the only conceivable way of viewing the world, are by that token authoritarian and ideological. It is one of the functions of ideology to 'naturalise' social reality, to make it seem as innocent and unchangeable as nature itself."[19] Barthes is linking Saussurian linguistics with a Marxist interpretation of ideology that sees bourgeois thought as concealing the true conditions of social existence.

Thus in *Mythologies* Barthes treats the relation between signifier and signified at the level of denotation as that between the arbitrary signifier and the *given* signified. The "object-language," or denotative language, involves a premythic signification process in which there is a presupposed natural link between the signifier and signified that constitutes the denotative sign. It is only at the level of "connotation" that this is seen as constitutive of the signified.[20] In Barthes's later work, this distinction collapses, as does the distinction between object-language and metalanguage. The semiology of *Mythologies* uses as part of the process of demythification the creation of a metalanguage, which, Rosalind Coward and John Ellis argue, unveils the systematic nature of another language. What happens is that "the language analysed is placed in the position of a signified, re-presented by the metalanguage." But this method no longer works when the primacy of the signifier within signification is acknowledged and "signification then appears to be a productivity (which presupposes the production of certain positions for the speaking subject), rather than a system that can be operated, or 'summed up' in a metalanguage by a transcendent subject."[21] Of course this brings the problem of subjectivity back in. Ideology is now seen as entering into the very constitution of every sign, and the whole sign system, not just connotation, is exposed in its complicity with specific forms of society.

THE UNCONSCIOUS

If Saussure broke with the idea of language as a tool to express thoughts about reality and pointed to how the speaking subject was thoroughly embedded in an always already preexisting language system, Freud questioned the idea of the rational, accessible character of thought itself. In so doing he posed another challenge to the concept of the subject implicit in Cartesian philosophy, with its understanding of consciousness as primary. For Freud, "the division of the psychical into what is conscious and what is unconscious is the fundamental premise of psychoanalysis. . . . Psychoanalysis cannot situate the essence of the psychical in consciousness, but is obliged to regard consciousness as a quality of the psychical, which may be present in addition to other qualities or may be absent."[22] He recognized the radical nature of this proposition to the Cartesian position: "To most people who have been educated in philosophy the idea of anything psychical which is not also conscious is so inconceivable that it seems to them absurd and refutable simply by logic."[23]

Yet Freud's departure has now been accepted and our view of the subject revised. From a Freudian perspective, consciousness is a particular aspect of the unconscious and not the most general feature of the "mind":

The unconscious is the larger sphere, which includes within it the smaller sphere of the conscious. Everything conscious has an unconscious preliminary stage; whereas what is unconscious may remain at that stage and nevertheless claim to be regarded as having the full value of a psychical process. The unconscious is the true psychical reality; *in its innermost nature it is as much unknown to us as the reality of the external world, and it is as incompletely presented by the data of consciousness as is the external world by the communications of our sense organs.*[24]

This relationship is represented in what is called Freud's "first topography." Two theories of the "agencies" or "instances" of the psychical apparatus can be found in Freud. The first topography distinguishes the unconscious, preconscious, and conscious (Table 2.1), the second the id, superego, and ego (Table 2.2). Whereas the unconscious is formed from repressed wishful impulses and is incapable of becoming conscious in itself, the preconscious contains latent thoughts that can become conscious. Descriptively, of course, neither unconscious nor preconscious is part of consciousness.

Table 2.1   Freud's First Topography

Psychical Processes		
Conscious	Preconscious	Unconscious
Conscious thoughts	Latent thoughts	Repressed thoughts
Controlled by the reality principle	Controlled by the reality principle	Wishful impulses driven by the pleasure principle
Secondary processes	Secondary processes	Primary processes
Linked to organs of perception	Capable of becoming conscious	Not capable of becoming conscious in itself

Table 2.2   Freud's Second Topography

Ego	Superego (Ego-Ideal)	Id
Intermediary between id and external world	Like the conscience	Store of drives
Part preconscious, part unconscious		Unconscious

There is overlap between the two topographies. Both involve dynamic relationship and conflict between the agencies. But the role of the ego is not clear in the first topography.[25] Freud conceived of it in a new way with the introduction of the concept of narcissism. He did not see a unified ego as present from birth, but as having to be developed, though he does not specify just how this happens. Lacan's mirror stage gives an account that fills the gap, as we shall see in Chapter 5.

The study of dreams can give us insight into unconscious processes.[26] As Freud was at pains to explain, however, this insight is derived not directly, from an examination of the *content* of dreams, but indirectly, from an account of their *form*. There are two aspects to the interpretation of dreams: a practical task and a theoretical task. It is important to begin by making the distinction between the manifest dream and the latent dream thoughts. The practical task of dream interpretation is to transform a dream's manifest content, as recounted by the analysand, into the latent dream thoughts: "The dream-thoughts and the dream-content are presented to us like two versions of the same subject-matter in two different languages. . . . The dream-content . . . is expressed as it were in a pictographic script, the characters of which have to be transposed individually into the language of dream-thoughts."[27]

When we have identified, through the patient's associations, the latent dream-thoughts, we still have not arrived at the nub of the dream. The theoretical task, undertaken by the theory of the dream process, is to explain the hypothetical dream-work.[28] Latent dream thoughts are often just the residues of the day—they are not unconscious or repressed but preconscious. Freud concluded from his work, however, that in every dream an instinctual wish or unconscious impulse was represented as fulfilled, and that this is the true creator of the dream.

What is of interest in psychoanalysis and psychoanalytic theory is the process through which this happens, which Freud calls "dream-work." The mechanisms of the process include condensation and compression, displacement, and representation. It is through a study of the process of dream-work that an understanding of the unconscious motivator of the dream can be gained. Again, the secret of the dream is not in the content but in the form, the process through which the content is produced. The processes Freud described for dream-work recur in many discussions of ideology, subjectivity, and the social or symbolic order, so I discuss them briefly.

Condensation and compression occur when one element in the manifest dream corresponds to numerous dream-thoughts or vice versa, where one element is represented by several images: "Not only are the elements of a dream determined by the dream-thoughts many times over, but the individual dream thoughts are represented in the dream by several elements."[29] The elements of a dream around which many associations converge are overdetermined; in other words, their presence in the manifest dream does not rely on just one link. As Freud puts it:

> Elements found their way into the content of the dream because they possessed copious contacts with the majority of the dream-thoughts, because, that is to say, they constituted "nodal points" upon which a great number of dream-thoughts converged, and because they had several meanings in connection with the interpretation of the dream. The explanation of this . . . can also be put in another way: each of the elements of the dream's content turns out to have been *"overdetermined"*—to have been represented in the dream-thoughts many times over.[30]

The dream thoughts are "interwoven" at these points.

The second process, displacement, or a shifting of accent, takes place when important elements in the dream thoughts are displaced by less important elements, which then receive a more central place in the manifest dream. "The dream is, as it were, differently centered from the dream-thoughts—its content has different elements as its central point."[31] This produces dream-distortion: "The consequence of this is that the dream-content no longer resembles the core of the dream-thoughts and that the dream gives no more than a distortion of the dream-wish which exists in the unconscious."[32] It is in this way that the dream-wishes can escape the "censorship" of resistance and find expression in the dream content. Displacements can involve the replacement of one particular idea by another closely associated with it or can be combined with condensation, whereby two elements are replaced with an intermediate one. Another source of displacement can occur in a change in the verbal expression. "Words, since they are the nodal points of numerous ideas, may be regarded as predestined to ambiguity, [and dreams] make unashamed use of the advantages thus offered by words for purposes of condensation and disguise."[33] Freud's work also points to the same occurrence in jokes and witticisms.

So there is an interplay of these three factors of displacement, condensation, and overdetermination in the construction of dreams through the process of dream work. A further factor that Freud considers is representation. Dreams are a particular form of the representation of thought. Dream thoughts are transformed into a collection of sensory images and visual scenes.[34] Subtle relations of thought are dropped because they cannot be represented, and symbols are used for concrete versions of abstract terms. Other changes take place, such as the representation of temporal relations as spatial ones. Logical connections between dream-thoughts are represented in a variety of ways, for example, by simultaneity in time. Relations of similarity, consonance, or approximation are represented by unification—for example, "identification" (with people) is represented by a person's having the name of one individual but the features of another, contradiction may be expressed by a reversal, and so on. Representation by symbols is also common: "This symbolism is not peculiar to dreams, but is characteristic of unconscious ideation. . . . It is to be found in folklore, and in popular myths, legends, linguistic idioms, proverbial wisdom and current jokes."[35] As well as condensation and displacement, a further factor in dream work is whether something is representable in any of these ways. A final, optional factor is what Freud calls "secondary revision," the process of filling in gaps and introducing connections to make the dream appear more rational. Part of the process of "censorship," it makes the dream seem more intelligible, and less absurd and disconnected.

The evasion of censorship is crucial for Freud in explaining why it is that dream work takes such a different form from waking thought. The differences are striking, but "at bottom, dreams are nothing other than a particular *form* of thinking. . . . It is the *dream-work* that creates the form,"[36] and it is this, and not the latent dream thoughts, that is the essence of dreaming. Dreams are just another attempt "at solving the problems by which our mental life is faced."[37]

FEMINIST DESTABILIZATIONS

Feminist theorists have found Freud's work notoriously problematic, and his adoption by some feminists is controversial. His earliest work on psychoanalysis was with women hysterics, and he has been accused of producing a theory that relies on, exploits, and perpetuates a particular notion of woman as subject. The work of other theorists I consider in this book has also had an ambivalent reception by feminists.[38] But the contribution made by feminism, gender studies, and queer theory to the decentering of the subject should be seen more broadly, not "merely" as critique. Feminist theorizing has been crucial in decentering the Cartesian subject. Whereas Saussure's challenge to the picture of language as individual and Freud's elaboration of the significance and distinctiveness of unconscious thought have pointed to the problems with a notion of a rational, thinking individual, feminism has challenged another aspect of the Cartesian subject: its disembodied, sexless, and gender-blind character. This has in turn gone alongside wider challenges to the Cartesian subject's claim, as white, Western, heterosexual male, to a position of neutral universality.

To gain an understanding of the feminist decentering of the subject, I examine the work of Luce Irigaray.[39] Irigaray's intervention, in *Speculum of the Other Woman,*[40] begins with a trenchant, and very funny, deconstruction of Freud's writings on femininity (entitled "The Blind Spot of an

Old Dream of Symmetry") and ends with an equally amusing reading of Plato's cave (*antre*) as womb (*ventre*).[41] Irigaray's mocking of Freud is merciless. In his search for an infallible method of discrimination between the sexes, whether in anatomy or psychology, Freud flounders regularly, as Irigaray delights in showing us. Freud notes that there are variations in secondary sexual characteristics. Irigaray remarks that we should perhaps then "display some caution before claiming to belong to one sex or the other." She then calls for seriousness and redirects us to Freud and what she calls his "scientific certainties." She quotes his statement that "only one kind of sexual *product*—ova or semen—is nevertheless present in one person." But as she then recalls, Freud equivocates yet again: This is true "apart, alas, from 'the very rarest of cases.'" She concludes: "All this, certainly, is very embarrassing."[42]

For Irigaray, Freud's importance is that he brought to light "the sexual indifference that underlies the truth of any science, the logic of every discourse."[43] Yet he does not escape phallogocentrism: He sees not two sexes but only one.[44] He describes the female always in terms of a deficiency in relation to the male, overlooking any possibility of a specificity for the female sex.

Speculum was written in the early 1970s, when the women's movement and "women's liberation" that had surfaced alongside other social movements after 1968 were flourishing. Women's liberation had to go "beyond simply a quest for equality between the sexes," a demand that presupposes a neutral point of comparison.[45] The dominance of one form of subjectivity, projected as universal, arises from "*the decline of sexual culture [which] goes hand in hand with* the establishment of different values which are supposedly universal but turn out to entail *one part of humanity having a hold over the other,* here the world of men over that of women."[46] It is not just a question of equal treatment of women, or even the recognition of woman's perspective as different, but a matter of the reinstatement of a whole economy of sexuality that has been erased. Woman has become "the non-masculine," not a different gender but "an abstract nonexistent reality."[47] In other words, "being a woman is equated with not being a man."[48] What is lost is "sexed subjective identity," and this is reflected in language and in culture that perpetuates "the pseudo-neutrality of those laws and traditions that privilege masculine genealogies and their codes of logic."[49] Irigaray's own work is "an attempt to create a new cultural era: that of sexual difference."[50] What this means is elaborated in the way *Speculum* criticizes "the exclusive right of the use(s), exchange(s), representation(s) of one sex by the other"; it involves the entry of "the sexed body" into theorizations of subjectivity and culture.[51]

The task Irigaray sets herself is immense, as she admits; the possibility of a "feminist" critique is limited and constrained by language itself and its phallogocentrism. Women cannot speak as women. They are defined as "object" in relation to the male "subject." The patriarchal structure of language excludes them:

> From a feminine locus nothing can be articulated without a questioning of the symbolic itself. But we do not escape so easily from reversal. We do not escape, in particular, by thinking we can dispense with a rigorous interpretation of phallogocentrism. There is no simple manageable way to leap to the outside of phallogocentrism, *nor any possible way to situate oneself there, that would result from the simple fact of being a woman.*[52]

This is the necessity that inspired *Speculum,* the need to take a trajectory backward through Western philosophy, which Irigaray calls "our cultural imaginary," or "the 'masculine' imaginary,"[53] which is the same thing. This attempt to move backward has two purposes. First, it allows Irigaray to delineate a possible "outside" to the masculine imaginary; second, it allows her to situate herself "with respect to it as a woman, implicated in it and at the same time exceeding its limits." This excess is crucial—and the reaction to it is laughter. Irigaray asks: "Isn't laughter the first form of liberation from a secular oppression? *Isn't the phallic tantamount to the seriousness of meaning?*"[54] She suggests that it is in laughter that the phallic can be contested or resisted:

> To escape from a pure and simple reversal of the masculine position means in any case not to forget to laugh. Not to forget that the dimension of desire, of pleasure, is untranslatable, unrepresentable, irrecuperable, in the "seriousness"—the adequacy, the univocity, the truth . . . —of a discourse that claims to state its meaning. Whether it is produced by men or women.[55]

She is not saying by this that "one has to give in to saying just anything at all." Rather, she argues that it is the articulation of a discourse that lays claim to truth, singularity, and seriousness of meaning that conceals the violence of phallogocentrism and, what is more important, its political force: "*Speaking the truth constitutes the prohibition on woman's pleasure, and thus on the sexual relation.* The covering up of its forcefulness, of force itself, under the lawmaking power of discourse."[56]

Irigaray's work calls for a view of the subject as necessarily embodied; this destabilizes the abstractions of the Cartesian subject. Judith Butler, though she, too, wants to direct our attention to embodied subjects, warns against "an easy return to the *materiality* of the body or the materiality of sex." According to Butler, "to invoke matter is to invoke a sedimented history of sexual hierarchy and sexual erasures which should surely be an *object* of feminist inquiry, but which would be quite problematic as a *ground* of feminist theory" or of a feminist rethinking of subjectivity.[57] For Butler, "the very formation of 'sex' and its 'materiality'" is an instance of power relations at work.[58] Butler calls for an examination of the conditions under which the materiality of the body is formed and in particular the way this takes place through categories of sex. In other words, she wants a "return to matter as a *sign* which in its redoublings and contradictions enacts an inchoate drama of sexual difference."[59] What she is arguing for is a problematization of the materiality of the body as a presupposition, and a challenging of the presumption of "constructedness and materiality as necessarily oppositional notions."[60] "Matter" or "materiality" must be reexamined. A loss of epistemological certainty may result, but "such a loss of certainty is not the same as political nihilism. On the contrary, such a loss may well indicate a significant and promising shift in political thinking. This unsettling of 'matter' can be understood as initiating new possibilities, new ways for bodies to matter."[61]

In a sense, feminism's first destabilization was that of the dichotomous thinking upon which notions of "materiality" as opposed to "constructedness," as well as the Cartesian subject, are based; feminism, through a concern with the way the separation and hierarchization of man/woman works to install a particular type of thinking, is sensitive to the function of other dichotomies: inside/outside, mind/body, doubt/certainty, rational/irrational, public/private, and so forth. The elaboration of a Cartesian subjectivity relies on these dichotomies. Escaping this way of thinking is not easy. Irigaray's critique runs the risk of continuing dichotomization by her emphasis on the feminine. Butler, for example, believes Irigaray is guilty of "idealising and appropriating the 'elsewhere' as the feminine." Butler asks: "What is the 'elsewhere' of Irigaray's 'elsewhere'? If the feminine is not the only or primary kind of being that is excluded from the economy of masculinist reason, what and who is excluded in the course of Irigaray's analysis?"[62] Irigaray's work risks reproducing the dichotomies it seeks to subvert. Like feminists who adopt a notion of a particular female standpoint or a feminine ethic or those who claim equality for "women," this position inverts the hierarchy man/woman, rather than displacing it. I return to these problems in Chapter 4, where I reexamine the political impact of problematizations of gender difference and the way gendered subjectivities are constituted. As Butler herself remarks, however, the critique of a term such as "woman" does not mean that it can no longer be used politically: "It must be possible both to use the term, to use it tactically even as one is, as it were, used and positioned by it, and also to subject the term to a critique."[63]

SOCIAL BEING

As we have seen, Saussure questions the notion of language as a neutral tool, used by the speaking subject to express preexisting thoughts and to allocate names to objects in the world. He introduces instead a picture of language as always already there before the subject and beyond the control of subjects as individuals. Marx extends this approach beyond language as such, claiming that social action takes place against the background of social structures that preexist the individual as agent. Marxism's displacement of the Enlightenment subject from the center of the world comes with the contention that "men" make history, but not in circumstances of their own choosing. It is these preexisting circumstances, the social conditions into which the subject is born, that set the framework for action. Moreover, the crucial claim is that it is action that determines consciousness, not consciousness that determines social being: "The mode of production of material life conditions the social, political and intellectual life. . . . It is not the consciousness of men that determines their being, but, on the contrary, their social being that determines their consciousness."[64]

For Marx, material relations are at the root of the social and in each historical era produce forms of consciousness that reflect in some way the specific material forms of that period. Marx claims that "legal relations as well as forms of state are to be grasped neither from themselves nor from the so-called general development of the human mind, but rather have their roots in the material conditions of life,"[65] that is, in what is called "civil society" or "political economy." This is the base-superstructure model of the social. Here material economic relations form the foundation and ideas, rational thought, and such like are seen not as the independent product of rational, conscious Cartesian subjects but as arising, more or less directly, as a superstructure built on the economic base. Marx considers relations of production as central to the concept of the "base." It is the "total of these relations of production [that] constitutes the economic structure of society, the real foundation, on which rises a legal and political superstructure and to which correspond definite forms of social consciousness."[66]

The Cartesian subject has been displaced, not by positing an unconscious underlying the subject's consciousness, as in Freud, but by arguing that consciousness itself is not what it appears. It is not independent but linked to social structures. Moreover, historical progress is no longer to be seen as arising from increasing human enlightenment but from the development of the material productive forces of society. It is when the legal structure and state forms become inappropriate for the productive forces at their new stage of development that a period of social revolution begins and "with the change of the economic foundations the entire immense superstructure is more or less rapidly transformed."[67] We cannot think what we choose—our position in the social structure and the nature of that structure in terms of the predominant mode of production dictate (more or less) what our ideas will be.

Debates have taken place within Marxism about the determinism implied in the concept of ideology as superstructural and in that sense secondary to the economic base.[68] The argument that the economic should be seen as determining only "in the last instance" is an attempt to resolve the issue. It is conceded that elements of the superstructure (the state, for example, or the ideological) can have a "relative autonomy" from the economic. In his structural theory of social formations, Althusser identifies three levels of practice: economic, political, and ideological. Each has its own rhythm of development and change. The ideological cannot be read off from the economic or vice versa. Under particular historical circumstances, an articulation between these relatively autonomous practices can produce an overdetermination. If ideology is seen as a set of practices, it can be regarded as being maintained and reproduced by what Althusser calls ideological state apparatuses (ISAs): schools, the family, and so on. The development of historical forces takes place in part with the ideological dominance of the ruling class reproduced through the mechanisms of the ISAs. In his work on interpellation, Althusser explores how ideologies come to be effective: how subjects are "recruited" to ideological positions. He is concerned with how ideologies operate through the unconscious as representations of the imaginary relations of individuals to their real conditions of existence. He proposes that they construct us as subjects by a mechanism of interpellation or hailing, which simultaneously names and positions the subject.

An alternative, less deterministic reading of Marxism sees history not as driven by the independent development of the productive forces but by class struggle.[69] Each mode of production brings along with it certain social classes, defined by their relationship to the means of production. In capitalism, for example, ownership of the means of production rests with the bourgeoisie, who form the ruling class. The working class is the exploited class—its members are forced to sell their labor to the owners of the means of production in exchange for wages. Because their interests in the productive process are opposed, an antagonism between the two classes results and eventually leads to class conflict and class struggle, with revolution and the overthrow of capitalism as the outcome. In each epoch the ruling ideas will be the ideas of the ruling class. The ideology of capitalism, for example, is bourgeois ideology. In this view, ideas have a strong "class-belongingness."

Of course this account presents the approach very simplistically. Marx does, even in his more "determinist" stance, distinguish carefully between the material changes in the economic conditions of production, which can be determined "exactly," and the transformation of the "ideological forms." The implication is that the latter are more indeterminate. Struggle is involved even in this version of Marx's position; transformation is not automatic. In Marx's words: "A distinction should always be made between the material transformation of the economic conditions of production, which can be determined with the precision of natural science, and the legal, political, religious, aesthetic or philosophic—in short, ideological forms in which men become conscious of this conflict and fight it out."[70]

Antonio Gramsci's analysis of ideology and ideological hegemony is crucial in understanding how class and class struggle might operate in practice.[71] If the motor of change is class struggle, we encounter the problem of "class consciousness" and the constitution of social class. Ideology enters the debate in a different way, as "false consciousness." As long as it accepts the "ruling" bourgeois ideology, the proletariat is considered misled as to its true interests. Another way of saying this is that the working class is not constituted as a class *in and for itself* until it overcomes "false consciousness" to become aware of its *real* class interests. But if the ruling ideas of an epoch are determined by the economic base, how can the working class ever become aware of its real interests as a class? Gramsci tackles some of these problems, introducing into the debate notions of hegemony and organic ideology.

There are several distinctive features of Gramsci's approach to ideology. First, ideology has a material existence: It is not just ideas or consciousness but embodied in institutions and apparatuses. It is not merely "superstructural." Second, Gramsci gives the elements that are articulated and rearticulated no necessary class belonging. Gramsci puts forward the concept of an organic ideology, one that is deeply rooted in a society. Ideologies define the terrain on which people struggle and produce action. To work, ideologies are experienced through the subject. Organic ideologies are tied up with common sense, the spontaneous philosophy of the people. They draw on commonsense meanings, and this link gives them roots and depth. It gives them a taken-for-granted, natural quality. Common sense, which Gramsci sees in language, in what counts as good sense, and in popular folklore, contains stratified deposits or traces of all previous philosophical systems. There is a continual complex process of transformation and interaction among philosophy, common sense, and folklore. Political ideas become organic by being absorbed into the structure of common sense.

Gramsci regards the self as a product of this historical process, which "has deposited . . . an infinity of traces, without leaving an inventory."[72] The process is an unconscious one. But philosophy cannot be divorced from politics; a conception of the world is a political matter. Organic ideologies are an active material force and to become effective they must be organized. We must look at how ideas circulate and who controls the process, how intellectuals are formed and their role, and the relations of power that accompany the dominance or contestation of ideas. Gramsci's analysis gives a strong political dimension to the operation of ideological constructions in the world. He sees their contestation as a long process of struggle from the bottom up and a powerful tool for political change. His analysis moves away from Marxist class-belongingness of ideas. There is no single dominant ideology but a coexistence of many different currents within a discursive formation. This approach gives a central role to the notion that through gaining hegemony a particular ideological position and the group linked to it become powerful. Through processes of contestation, elements can be rearticulated around different ideological positions and new hegemonies can arise.

CONCLUSION

In this chapter I have discussed four of Hall's "decenterings": those of Saussure, Freud, feminism, and Marx. The linguistics of Saussure challenged the picture of language as a neutral tool used to express preexisting thoughts or to name objects that were already there. In contrast, *language* is always already there—preexisting the individual or the object as a social structure where meaning depends on processes beyond the subject. In Hall's phrase, we no longer speak language—*language speaks us*. Freudian psychoanalysis questioned the rational subject at its roots, challenging the view of thought itself as something the individual has access to or control over. Freud shows that to account for dreams we must suppose an unconscious, and that this unconscious was a more significant part of "mental processes" than conscious thought. This radically challenged the Cartesian view that knowledge of oneself as a thinking being was the solution to doubt. Feminism raised the issue of the subject as sexed and embodied; a view that ignores this claims a neutrality and universality for the masculine that feminist theorizing has called into question. It also problematizes the neglect of issues of "race," ethnicity, and sexuality in discussions of the subject, pointing to the white, Western, heterosexual male nature of the Cartesian subject. Finally, Marx locates the center of conscious being not in mental processes but in social activity. It is social processes that produce thought, not the other way around. Althusser and Gramsci both theorize the processes involved, Althusser looking at interpellation as a way in which subjects are recruited to particular subject positions and Gramsci exploring the production of organic ideologies that command the support of a hegemonic bloc and articulate a number of ideological elements.

The rational, Enlightenment subject, enunciated specifically in Cartesian philosophy as the basis of the distinction between "truth" and "illusion," has been displaced from its central position and problematized, and the notions of truth and illusion have themselves come under scrutiny as ideology is examined. In Chapters 4–6, I show how the four decenterings of the subject I have discussed here are drawn upon and elaborated by Derrida, Lacan, and Žižek. I look at Hall's fifth decentering, by Foucault, in Chapter 3.

NOTES

1. René Descartes, *Discourse on Method and Other Writings,* trans. F. E. Sutcliffe (Harmondsworth, UK: Penguin, 1968), 53–54.
2. Stuart Hall, "The Question of Cultural Identity," in *Modernity and Its Futures,* ed. Stuart Hall, David Held, and Tony McGrew (London: Polity, in association with the Open University, 1992), 275.
3. Ibid., 276.
4. Ibid., 273–325.
5. Ferdinand de Saussure, *Course in General Linguistics,* trans. Wade Baskin (New York: McGraw-Hill, 1966), 14.
6. Ibid., 156.
7. Ibid., 71.
8. Ibid., 71.
9. Ibid., 87.
10. Ibid., 114.
11. Ibid., 116.
12. Ibid., 120.
13. Ibid., 121.
14. Ibid., 130.
15. Françoise Gadet, *Saussure and Contemporary Culture,* trans. Gregory Elliot (London: Hutchinson Radius, 1989), 12.
16. Rosalind Coward and John Ellis, *Language and Materialism: Developments in Semiology and the Theory of the Subject* (London: Routledge & Kegan Paul, 1977), 3.
17. Gadet, *Saussure,* 154–155.
18. Roland Barthes, *Mythologies,* trans. Annette Lavers (London: Jonathan Cape, 1972).
19. Terry Eagleton, *Literary Theory: An Introduction* (Oxford: Blackwell, 1983), 135.
20. Coward and Ellis, *Language and Materialism,* 29.
21. Ibid., 32.
22. Sigmund Freud, "The Ego and the Id," in *On Metapsychology: The Theory of Psychoanalysis,* ed. Angela Richards, trans. James Strachey (Harmondsworth, UK: Penguin, 1984), 351.
23. Ibid., 351.
24. Sigmund Freud, *The Interpretation of Dreams,* trans. James Strachey (Harmondsworth, UK: Penguin, 1991), 773.
25. Bice Benvenuto and Roger Kennedy, *The Works of Jacques Lacan: An Introduction* (London: Free Association Books, 1986), 49.
26. And indeed it was this study among others that led Freud to postulate the unconscious. Sigmund Freud, *The Complete Introductory Lectures on Psychoanalysis,* trans. James Strachey (London: George Allen and Unwin, 1971); Freud, *Interpretation of Dreams.*

27. Freud, *Interpretation of Dreams,* 381.

28. Freud, *Complete Introductory Lectures,* 474.

29. Freud, *Interpretation of Dreams,* 389.

30. Ibid., 388–389.

31. Ibid., 414.

32. Ibid., 417.

33. Ibid., 456.

34. Ibid., 484.

35. Ibid., 468.

36. Ibid., 650.

37. Ibid.

38. For discussions of this, see, for example, Diane Elam, *Feminism and Deconstruction: Ms. en Abyme* (London: Routledge, 1994); Ellen K. Feder, Mary C. Rawlinson, and Emily Zakin, eds., *Derrida and Feminism: Recasting the Question of Woman* (London: Routledge, 1997); Elizabeth Grosz, *Jacques Lacan: A Feminist Introduction* (London: Routledge, 1990); Lois McNay, *Foucault and Feminism: Power, Gender and the Self* (Cambridge: Polity, 1992); Juliet Mitchell, *Psychoanalysis and Feminism* (Harmondsworth, UK: Penguin, 1974); Juliet Mitchell and Jacqueline Rose, *Feminine Sexuality: Jacques Lacan and the École Freudienne,* trans. Jacqueline Rose (New York: Norton, 1985); Renata Salecl, *The Spoils of Freedom: Psychoanalysis and Feminism After the Fall of Socialism* (London: Routledge, 1994).

39. I could have chosen other theorists. Julia Kristeva is an obvious contender; her work provides particularly telling developments of both linguistics (see, for example, Julia Kristeva, *Revolution in Poetic Language,* trans. Margaret Waller [New York: Columbia University Press, 1984]) and subjectivity (for example, in Julia Kristeva, *Strangers to Ourselves,* trans. Leon S. Roudiez [New York: Columbia University Press, 1991]). A helpful introduction to French feminisms, including Irigaray and Kristeva, is given in Elizabeth Grosz, *Sexual Subversions: Three French Feminists* (St. Leonards, Australia: Allen & Unwin, 1989). Kristeva and Irigaray are compared and contrasted in Elizabeth Grosz, *Jacques Lacan: A Feminist Introduction* (London: Routledge, 1990), chapter 6.

40. Luce Irigaray, *Speculum of the Other Woman,* trans. Gillian C. Gill (Ithaca, NY: Cornell University Press, 1985). This book was originally published in French in 1974, but it was more than ten years before the English translation appeared.

41. But she refuses the notion of the book's "beginning" or "ending"; see Luce Irigaray, *This Sex Which Is Not One,* trans. Catherine Porter, with Carolyn Burke (Ithaca, NY: Cornell University Press, 1985), 68.

42. Irigaray, *Speculum,* 15.

43. Irigaray, *This Sex Which Is Not One,* 69.

44. The term "phallogocentrism" combines logocentrism and the concept of the phallus. The notion of logocentrism derives from Derrida's work on the specificity of Western philosophic discourse, particularly in its use of dichotomous reasoning and a metaphysics that valorizes presence (Chapter 4). The phallus as a concept from psychoanalysis expresses the symbolic order as founded by patriarchy.

45. Luce Irigaray, *Je, Tu, Nous: Toward a Culture of Difference,* trans. Alison Martin (New York: Routledge, 1993), 11.

46. Ibid., 16.

47. Ibid., 20.

48. Ibid., 71.

49. Ibid., 53.

50. Ibid., 52.

51. Ibid., 59.

52. Irigaray, *This Sex Which Is Not One,* 162.

53. Ibid., 162.

54. Ibid., 163.

55. Ibid.

56. Ibid.

57. Judith Butler, *Bodies That Matter: On the Discursive Limits of 'Sex'* (London: Routledge, 1993), 49.

58. Ibid., 16–17.

59. Ibid., 49.

60. Ibid., 28.

61. Ibid., 30.

62. Ibid., 49.

63. Ibid., 29.

64. Karl Marx, "Preface to 'A Contribution to the Critique of Political Economy,'" in *Karl Marx: Selected Writings,* ed. David McLellan (Oxford: Oxford University Press, 1977), 181.

65. Ibid., 181.

66. Ibid.

67. Ibid., 182.

68. There are a number of discussions of the various views within Marxism; see, for example, Michèle Barrett, *The Politics of Truth: From Marx to Foucault* (Cambridge: Polity, 1991); David McLellan, *Ideology,* 2nd ed. (Buckingham, UK: Open University Press, 1995); and Jorge Larrain, *The Concept of Ideology* (London: Hutchinson, 1979). These debates are well rehearsed, so I do not consider them in any detail here.

69. This is the view attributed to the *Communist Manifesto.* Karl Marx and Frederick Engels, "The Communist Manifesto," in *Karl Marx: Selected Writings,* ed. David McLellan (Oxford: Oxford University Press, 1977), 221–247.

70. Marx, "Preface," 182.

71. For a discussion of this, see, for example, James Donald and Stuart Hall, *Politics and Ideology* (Milton Keynes, UK: Open University Press, 1986), xi–xiv.

72. Antonio Gramsci, *Selections from Prison Notebooks,* ed. and trans. Quintin Hoare and Geoffrey Nowell Smith (London: Lawrence and Wishart, 1971), 324.

3

Foucault's Docile Bodies

Assumptions of a centered, preexisting subject are crucial for modern notions of "politics," as we saw in Chapter 1: Unsettling these preconceptions is a first step toward a return of "the political." Michel Foucault's work continues the decentering of the subject discussed in the previous chapter. In that chapter we saw how the language of thought was problematized. For Foucault, not only is the subject's participation in language reversed in that "language speaks the subject," but processes of self-discipline are not what they appear. They are historically contingent as part of discursive practices; more than that though, they are produced by and serve power relations so that "the soul is the prison of the body." Indeed, Foucault's analysis of the subject as produced by disciplinary practices rather than just controlled by them leads to an account of the explicitly technologized, depoliticized subject of modernity.

Foucault's analysis of "relations of power" as decentralized and dispersed provides an alternative view of what might constitute "the political" as opposed to "politics." He puts forward a view of "power" not as something that can be "possessed" by some subjects, and then used to control other (also previously constituted) subjects but as something that, as "relations of power," is productive of subjects themselves. This productive or originating moment is parallel to what I discussed in Chapter 1 as "the political." Relations of power are productive of particular social forms. Furthermore, power is not the property of "politics": It is not centralized (in the state apparatus, for example) but dispersed. It is also to be regarded as intimately linked with resistance: Relations of power cannot occur without resistance. Foucault's analysis of the inseparability of discourse, the subject, and power plays a central part in the analysis of the political and processes of depoliticization or technologization.

Finally, Foucault's work on both discourse and ethics is important for an analysis of the political. His analysis of discourse as a "truth game" parallels recent work on ideology in what it attempts as well as the problems it encounters, despite his rejection of the *term* "ideology," which he associates with a specifically Marxist view of the separation between "truth" and "illusion." It enables us to analyze, through the concept of power/knowledge, how discursive practices, like other social practices, are "political." His examination of the ethics of existence gives us an approach to what the possibility of repoliticization might look like.

Commentators often separate Foucault's work into two periods: The first is concerned with "archaeology" sometimes presented as a variety of structuralism.[1] The second is based on a "genealogical" method.[2] Archaeology is seen as an analysis of discursive systems in themselves, genealogy as examining social practices as a whole, not the discursive realm alone, and specifically as being concerned with the role of power in the production of subjects. Although a concern with power and the political can be traced to his earliest books on madness, the contention made is that there is a break in Foucault's work. The *Birth of the Clinic* (first published in French in 1963), on clinical medicine, and *The Order of Things* (1996), an account of the rise of the human sciences, are seen as representative of his "archaeological" phase.[3] His later works, beginning with *Discipline and Punish* (1975), an account of prisons and disciplining practices, represent genealogy.[4] This chronology does not take into account his first work, on insanity, nor the final work, on techniques of the self.[5]

The break between archaeology and genealogy is often situated around the "Orders of Discourse," Foucault's inaugural lecture at the Collège de France in 1970.[6] His essay "Nietzsche, Genealogy, History" is also seen as an indicator of the new approach.[7] For Alan Sheridan, it marks the introduction of an explicit analysis of the power relations in discourse into Foucault's work: "This new realisation of the role of power in discourse was so important to Foucault that he felt impelled to abandon altogether the terms he had fashioned for himself [in the *Archaeology of Knowledge*] and to adopt . . . the Nietzschean term 'genealogy.'"[8] Power is a crucial element in genealogy that always remained at an implicit level in archaeology.

There is, however, a thread running through the whole of Foucault's work beginning with *Madness and Civilisation*. Foucault offers several accounts of his project, each with a different emphasis but each acknowledging the common thread. The first centers on the subject and modes of objectification that transform human beings into subjects: "The goal of my work . . . has not been to analyze the phenomenon of power. [It] has been to create a history of the different modes by which, in our culture, human beings are made subjects."[9] He identifies three modes of objectification that he has dealt with. The first is "the modes of inquiry which try to give themselves the status of sciences."[10] These include three: the speaking subject, studied in linguistics; the producing, laboring subject, studied in economics; and the subject as a living being, studied in biology. The second mode of objectification is "dividing practices"[11] that divide the subject within him- or herself or divide the subject from others, as in categorizing the mad and the sane, sick and healthy, criminal and noncriminal. Finally, he studies "the way a human being turns him- or herself into a subject, for example . . . as subjects of sexuality."[12]

In a second discussion, Foucault splits his work into three axes of genealogy: a truth axis, a power axis, and an ethics axis. In the slightly later work, "Genealogy of Ethics," Foucault describes different axes of genealogy around which he is articulating an ontology of the present:

> First, a historical ontology of ourselves in relation to truth through which we constitute ourselves as subjects of knowledge; second, a historical ontology of ourselves in relation to a field of power through which we constitute ourselves as subjects operating on others; third, a historical ontology in relation to ethics through which we constitute ourselves as moral agents.[13]

The axes of genealogy (truth, power, and ethics) parallel the modes of objectification (in the human sciences, dividing practices, and technologies of the self) discussed above.

In the third and final discussion, Foucault describes his work as a study of games of truth. This appears in the introduction to *The Use of Pleasure*, his penultimate book, published in 1984. Here Foucault accounts for the "theoretical shift" that has led him to rethink the volumes of the *History of Sexuality*.[14] He see this as his third theoretical shift. The first, directed at an analysis of the "advancement of learning," was to study the forms of discursive practices in the human sciences. The second, to analyze "power" (the move from archaeology to genealogy), was to a study of the "manifold relations, the open strategies, and the rational techniques that articulate the exercise of powers."[15] The third is a shift in order to analyze "the subject." As Foucault describes it: "After first studying the games of truth (*jeux de verité*) in their interplay with one another . . . and then studying their interaction with power relations . . . I felt obliged to study the games of truth in the relationship of self with self and the forming of oneself as subject."[16] These different "games of truth" clearly map onto Foucault's modes of objectification and axes of genealogy.

Despite these "shifts" from the study of one "game of truth" to another (and despite the description in terms of "games of truth," "axes of genealogy," or "modes of objectification"), in this discussion Foucault sees his work as a coherent whole, where both archaeology and genealogy contribute. He describes it as working toward a "history of truth": "Not a history that would be concerned with what might be true in the fields of learning, but an analysis of the 'games of truth,' the games of truth and error through which being is historically constituted as experience; that is as something that can and must be thought."[17] Both "archaeology" and "genealogy" have something to contribute to this "history of truth":

> It was a matter of analysing, not behaviours or ideas, nor societies and their "ideologies," but the *problematisations* through which being offers itself to be, necessarily, thought—and the *practices* on the basis of which these problematisations are formed. The archaeological dimension of the analysis made it possible to examine the forms themselves; its genealogical dimension enabled me to analyze their formation out of the practices and modifications undergone by the latter.[18]

In these terms, the elements of Foucault's particular practical studies can be redescribed: "There was the problematisation of madness and illness arising out of social and medical practices, and defining a certain pattern of 'normalisation'; a problematisation of life, language and labour in discursive practices that conformed to certain 'epistemic' rules; and a problematisation of crime and criminal behaviour emerging from certain punitive practices conforming to a 'disciplinary' model."[19] The final part of the jigsaw is his work, in *The Use of Pleasure* and *The Care of the Self,* on "how, in classical antiquity, sexual activity and sexual pleasures were problematised through practices of the self, bringing into play the criteria of an 'aesthetics of existence.'"[20]

His work on the truth axis, which I explore in the first section of the chapter, examines "discourse" as a political practice implicated in the production of subjects as "subjects of knowledge." He addresses the unity of "discursive formations" (where do we draw, or indeed *can* we draw, the boundaries of a discourse?), the production of subjects *in* discourse, and the more contentious and difficult question of the discursive/nondiscursive (which is often reduced to the question of whether there is a distinction to be made between "discourse" and "reality"). The issues involved here reverberate throughout this book: in Chapter 4 in my discussion of the *horstexte* in Derrida and again Chapter 5, where I examine Žižek's work on the retroactive operation of naming and the Lacanian "real."[21]

In the second section I turn to Foucault's second axis: power. The power axis is that aspect of Foucault's work that explores issues of depoliticization and technologization through the analysis of disciplinary techniques. First, I exemplify how Foucault uses "discourse" and "power" in his substantive work, by discussing parts of his writing on prisons and the carceral. This draws out insights into the technologization produced through disciplining practices and relates to notions of exclusionary practices first developed in *Madness and Civilisation.*[22] Second, I look at Foucault's notion of "power" and "power/knowledge" through a discussion of how power is always implicated in discourse and a review of Foucault's critique of "ideology." The link in Foucault between power and knowledge, or between power and discourse, is crucial in discussions of technologization and depoliticization. This link also incorporates an account of the subject. The relationship between knowledge and the social or political was in the past articulated by theories of ideology. I look briefly at Foucault's rejection of "ideology" and argue that his account of "games of truth" largely occupies the same terrain as that claimed by contemporary work on ideology.[23]

Finally, I examine the third axis: ethics. The ethics axis explores the subject's relation to itself, or in Foucault's terms the "technology of the self." What we consider to be ethics is historically contingent, not only in terms of the moral code that we follow but in the ways and means through which ethics is seen as possible in relation to the self. Foucault's work here leads him to a "political" position that advocates activism and vigilance as opposed to a "politics" of ultimate solutions.

DISCOURSE

In *The Order of Things,* Foucault argues that the human being as "subject" of knowledge is of recent origin. The human sciences (linguistics, economics, biology) that take "man" as their object did not arise, or were not instituted, to study a preexisting entity. Rather, "man," as the subject of science, was constituted in the process, through the birth of the human sciences. Thus "man" is not a timeless eternal being but is produced as a subject of knowledge, an object of science, through discursive practices. Of course as historically constituted, "man" as speaking, laboring, living subject can equally be obliterated, "like a face drawn in the sand at the edge of the sea."[24]

For Foucault, it is historically located practices, discourse among them, that as well as producing the "subject" as an entity produce exclusions and divisions—whether between a given society and its excluded other (as in *Madness and Civilisation,* where the excluded other is that which though interior is foreign and dangerous and hence has to be excluded)[25] or between "subjects of knowledge" within a culture (as in *The Order of Things*) or between the normal and the delinquent (as in *Discipline and Punish*).

But what is discourse? "Discourse is constituted by the difference between what one could say correctly at one period (under the rules of grammar and logic) and what is actually said."[26] Discourse is not a neutral, optional extra to the already existing "thing" or "thought." "In discourse something is formed, according to clearly definable rules . . . this something exists, subsists, changes, disappears, according to equally definable rules; in short . . . alongside everything a society can produce (alongside: that is to say in a determinate relationship with) there is the formation and transformation of 'things said.'"[27] Foucault sees his own work as writing the history of these "things said."

The study of discourse is distinct from the study of linguistics. Whereas linguistics examines the rules of language that underlie particular statements, "the description of the events of discourse poses a quite different question: how is it that one particular statement appeared rather than another?"[28] In other words, we can, linguistically, say many things. Why do we, in fact, say some things and not others? What he is concerned with is not *langue*, in Saussurian terms, but *parole:* not the language system but the particular enunciation. He also distinguishes the study of discourse from the history of thought, where the aim is to uncover meaning and intention behind statements. On the contrary, "a statement is always an event that neither the language nor the meaning can quite exhaust."[29] What Foucault undertakes to do is to describe the relations among statements and in particular, in *The Order of Things,* statements in discourses that involve the "sciences of man." He is seeking to elaborate the conditions of existence of discourses.

In *The Order of Things*, Foucault deliberately excludes any consideration of the relations of scientific discourse with "instruments, techniques, institutions, events, ideologies and interests."[30] The question of the relations between the "discursive" and the "nondiscursive" arises in *The Archaeology of Knowledge.* Two other closely related issues are also considered there: how to identify or define a discursive formation—how we can talk of the "same" discipline when no "essential" characteristic remains the same throughout change—and the relation of a discourse to its objects or subjects ("man" in the case of the human sciences).[31]

The question of the unity of discourse is one Foucault tackles at the beginning of *The Archaeology of Knowledge,* where he outlines some of the complexities of the enterprise: "How is one to specify the different concepts that enable us to conceive of discontinuity (threshold, rupture, break, mutation, transformation)? By what criteria is one to isolate the unities with which one is dealing; what is *a* science? What is an *oeuvre?* What is *a* theory? What is *a* concept? What is *a* text?"[32] He draws attention to the problems of generally accepted ways of resolving this—notions of tradition, for example. We need to question the notions of development and evolution, and the divisions and groupings we are familiar with: These are the very facts of discourse that are going to be analyzed. This includes even those "unities" that seem most obvious and immediate, like the book: "The frontiers of a book are never clear-cut: beyond the title, the first lines and the last full stop, beyond its internal configuration and its autonomous form, it is caught up in a system of references to other books, other texts, other sentences: it is a node within a network."[33]

The question of the objects of discourse is closely related to that of the unity of discourse, as we have seen: Objects are constituted and transformed in discourse. The aim of an archaeological approach is

> to substitute for the enigmatic treasure of "things" anterior to discourse, the regular formation of objects that emerge only in discourse. To define these objects without reference to the *ground,* the *foundation of things,* but by relating them to the body of rules that enable them to form as objects of a discourse and thus constitute the conditions of their historical appearance. To write a history of discursive objects that does not plunge them into the common depth of a primal soil, but deploys the nexus of regularities that govern their dispersion.[34]

Foucault's description of genealogy suggests a similar approach: Genealogy "opposes itself to the search for 'origins.'"[35] He characterized the latter as "an attempt to capture the exact essence of things, their purest possibilities, and their carefully protected identities, because [it] assumes the existence of immobile forms that precede the external world of accident and succession. This search is directed to 'that which was already there,' the image of a primordial truth."[36] Whereas the search for origins involves "the removal of every mask to ultimately disclose an original identity," the work of the genealogist finds something quite different: "not a timeless and essential secret, but the secret that [things] have no essence or that their essence was fabricated in a piecemeal fashion from alien forms."[37] The search for origins is ideological; it is based on a conception of birth as a moment of perfection, before the Fall, when things "emerged dazzling from the hands of a creator."[38]

The way in which discourses constitute their objects is crucial to an understanding of discourse itself, as opposed to language: Discourses are not "groups of signs (signifying elements referring to contents or representations) but . . . practices that systematically form the objects of which they speak."[39] Discourses are composed of signs, but "what they do is more than use these signs to designate things."[40] This is what makes them something more than language or speech.

Foucault does not set out a clear distinction between discursive and nondiscursive formations in the *Archaeology of Knowledge,*[41] though, as we have seen, he does distinguish between "discursive practices" and "other social practices" and speaks about the boundaries and limits of discursive formations. His study includes the whole play of dependencies—intradiscursive, interdiscursive, and extradiscursive. The latter are the relations "between discursive transformations and transformations outside discourse: for example the correlations studied in *Madness and Civilisation* and *Birth of the Clinic* between medical discourse and a whole play of economic, political and social changes."[42] This should be taken in the context of a view of the discursive as an "event." Foucault is not looking at codes, language, or the formal rules of discourse, nor at the subjects enunciating discourse, their consciousness or intention. He examines discursive events *as such,* in relation to other events, "discursive or otherwise."[43] The distinction between discursive and nondiscursive is a distinction between types of *event,* not between orders of being. Central to the debate, then, is that Foucault is not making the distinction often attributed to him between "ideas" or "language" and "reality." He is not setting up a division that implies discourse as separate in some sort of idealistic sense or in a sense that would invoke a base-superstructure distinction. He sees "discourse" as one practice among others, and he goes out of his way to stress its materiality.[44] His aim is an analysis of discourses in "the dimension of their exteriority," which means "to treat discourse . . . as a *monument* . . . to investigate . . . its conditions of existence . . . to relate the discourse not to thought, mind or subject which engendered it, but to the practical field in which it is deployed."[45]

His work is certainly designed to tackle the question of the relationship between discourse and other practices—political practices and scientific discourse, for example—even though *The Order of Things* specifically excludes this aspect. The relationship is not a simple, direct, causal one nor a question of parallel development. But the link is there, and the archaeology of discourse is designed to elucidate it. In the case of medicine, for example, "political practice did not transform the meaning or form of medical discourse, but the conditions of its emergence, insertion and functioning. . . . [But] the analysis becomes complex—these transformations in the conditions of existence and functioning of the discourse are not 'reflected,' 'transposed' or 'expressed' in the concepts, methods and utterances of medicine. They modify their rules of formation."[46] An analysis of this type of relationship (an interesting homology with the Freudian theory of dreams)[47] can "define how, to what extent, at what level discourses . . . can be objects of a political practice, and in what system of dependence they can exist in relation to it."[48] The relation between the discursive and the nondiscursive cannot be assumed; it must be the subject of historical analysis of how the discursive practice produces the institutional practice and vice versa, in a particular instance. The two do not exist in some "separate" way but are mutually constituted: "Theory does not express, translate or serve to apply practice: it is practice."[49]

DISCIPLINING PRACTICES

Foucault's work on the second axis of genealogy, the power axis, concerns modes of objectification called "dividing practices." I look in particular at the "disciplinary" model developed in *Discipline and Punish,* where

Foucault traces the emergence of the nineteenth-century prison system, which he calls the carceral. For Foucault, the prison does not represent something completely new; as a *form,* the procedure antedates its use in the penal system:

> The prison form . . . had already been constituted outside the legal apparatus when, throughout the social body, procedures were being elaborated for distributing individuals, fixing them in space, classifying them, extracting from them the maximum in time and forces, training their bodies, coding their continuous behaviour, maintaining them in perfect visibility, forming around them an apparatus of observation, registration and recording, constituting on them a body of knowledge that is accumulated and centralised.[50]

Once established, prison became the "self-evident" form of punishment, precisely because of the way it was bound up at a deep level with the functioning of society. This still holds a century later: "We are all aware of the inconveniences of prison and that it is dangerous when it is not useless. And yet one cannot 'see' how to replace it."[51]

There are two aspects to prison. Its use as a punishment is the first: Detention and the deprivation of liberty are based on a penalty that takes the form of wages. A certain amount of time is regarded as payment for the offense. This is what Foucault calls the judicioeconomic aspect. But the second aspect is the role of prison in transforming individuals. In this "it merely reproduces, with a little more emphasis, all the mechanisms that are to be found in the social body. . . . The prison is like a rather disciplined barracks, a strict school, a dark workshop, but not qualitatively different."[52] The transformation of individuals is the technicodisciplinary aspect of prison. Foucault stresses that from the start, in the early 1800s, prison had both these functions: "Penal imprisonment, from the beginning of the nineteenth century, covered both the deprivation of liberty and the technical transformation of individuals."[53]

The principles by which the technicodisciplinary aspect functions include isolation, work, and the modulation of the penalty or duration of imprisonment. Isolation is individualizing and provides solitude for reflection. It terminates any relation that is not between the individual and the hierarchy and that is not supervised by the authorities. Modulation of the duration of imprisonment can be used as an instrument of correction: It is adjusted to the transformation of prisoners during their terms. Work in prison is not only a reparation for the crime but an instrument of reform. Food-for-work programs, where those vulnerable to famine take part in "public works" in return for rations of food, operate on similar principles.[54]

The prison is the place where the inmate is under permanent observation and surveillance. Records are made and reports compiled regarding the prisoner's behavior, state of mind, improvement, and so on. It was for this reason that "the Panopticon—at once surveillance and observation, security and knowledge, isolation and transparency—found in the prison its privileged loci of realisation."[55] As opposed to the amphitheaters of a previous age, where large numbers of people could gather to watch a spectacle, the panopticon's design permits one person to supervise many, who are unable to see each other. The panopticon is "a prison-machine with a cell of visibility in which the inmate [is caught] and a central point from which a permanent gaze may control prisoners and staff."[56] This involves the expression of the disciplinary "form" in the architecture—the building. There is also a system of documentation, where individual reports on each prisoner are kept. The prison "has to extract unceasingly from the inmate a body of knowledge that will make . . . possible . . . a modification of the inmate that will be of use to society."[57] Foucault compares penal systems to accounting practices that ensure a return on capital: "Penitentiary practice produces a return on the capital invested in the penal system and in the building of heavy prisons."[58]

In the process, the prison is not so much concerned with the convict and the offense as with a rather different object—what Foucault calls "the delinquent": "The delinquent is to be distinguished from the offender by the fact that it is not so much his act as his life that is relevant in characterising him."[59] The individual is defined as a delinquent and criminology is made possible:

> The penitentiary technique and the delinquent are in a sense twin brothers. It is not true that it was the discovery of the delinquent through scientific rationality that introduced into our old prisons the refinement of penitentiary techniques. Nor is it true that the internal elaboration of penitentiary methods has finally brought to light the "objective" existence of a delinquency that the abstraction and rigidity of the law were unable to perceive. They appeared together, the one extending from the other, as a technological ensemble that forms and fragments the object to which it applies its instruments. . . . Delinquency is the vengeance of the prison on justice. It is a revenge formidable enough to leave the judge speechless. It is at this point that the criminologists raise their voices.[60]

This is a clear expression of how Foucault sees the subject and the knowledge of the subject, together with the institutional expression of that knowledge, as produced *together*. Once "delinquency" had given to criminal justice "a unitary field of objects, authenticated by the 'sciences,' and thus enabled it to function on a general horizon of 'truth,'"[61] the prison as an institution was not challenged. The "delinquent" is now taken into account when codes are written, when sentences are passed, and so on. "Justice" has been silenced in favor of criminology.

Despite all the efforts of criminologists and prison systems, the system fails: Delinquents reoffend and return to prison; the prison population does not decline but increases. Perhaps the continual failure of prison is part of the system. Foucault proposes that its role is not to "check" illegalities; on the contrary, "it differentiates them, it provides them with a general 'economy.'"[62] By branding the criminal and by maintaining a system that leads to repeat offenses, habitual offenders, and a criminal fraternity, what is produced serves not to eliminate crimes but to "distinguish them, to distribute them, to use them."[63] Foucault sees the penal system as part of an overall mechanism of domination, and the very failure of the system is central to its success. Foucault argues that this is the case: Prison succeeds in so far as it delineates a particular form of organized and organizable illegality: "Prison has succeeded very well in producing delinquency, a specific type, a politically or economically less dangerous—and, on occasion, usable—form of illegality; in producing delinquents, in an apparently marginal, but in fact centrally supervised milieu; in producing the delinquent as a pathologised subject."[64]

The function of the whole system (the police-prison-delinquency circuit) extends further, and its chief function, as Foucault points out, is depoliticization. It provides a means for surveillance that, though legitimized in terms of surveillance of delinquents, extends to whole populations; it is an agent for the colonization of illegality by the dominant groups. The chief task, however, remains that of separating "delinquents" from the bulk of the poorer classes, making it impossible for the link between illegality and political action, illegality and protest, to function. Political action that broke the law was and is regarded as "delinquent." Workers or other political activists are treated as criminals in prisons and denied political status.

This depoliticization involves a "normalizing power": "The judges of normality are present everywhere. We are in the society of the teacher-judge, the doctor-judge, the educator-judge, the 'social worker'-judge; it is on them that the universal reign of the normative is based."[65] This can be coupled with the rise of the human sciences. A particular way of capturing and observing the body is linked with "the involvement of definite relations of knowledge in relations of power; it called for a technique of overlapping subjection and objectification; it brought with it new procedures of individualisation. . . . Knowable man (soul, individuality, consciousness, conduct, whatever it is called) is the object-effect of this analytical investment, of this domination-observation."[66]

The mechanisms of normalization, depoliticization, and the proliferation of new disciplines produce

> subjected and practised bodies, "docile" bodies. Discipline increases the forces of the body (in economic terms of utility) and diminishes these

same forces (in political terms of obedience). In short, it dissociates power from the body. . . . If economic exploitation separates the force and the product of labour, let us say that disciplinary coercion establishes in the body the constricting link between an increased aptitude and an increased domination.[67]

Discipline creates particular types of "individuality": an individuality that is endowed with four characteristics: it is cellular (by the play of spatial distribution), it is organic (by the coding of activities), it is genetic (by the accumulation of time), it is combinatory (by the composition of forces). And, in doing so, it operates four great techniques: it draws up tables; it prescribes movements; it imposes exercises; lastly, in order to obtain the combination of forces, it arranges "tactics."[68]

As we saw in Chapter 1, mechanisms of normalization, technologization, and depoliticization can be seen in the practices of international relations. Processes of humanitarian intervention, development, securitization, diplomacy, democratization, and structural adjustment, for example, could all be analyzed in this way. Subjectivation, surveillance, and separation occur, with the agencies of development or global economic regulation (like the prisons) largely independent of any outside involvement. In a close parallel to Foucault's account, there is an ever increasing control that "organises into a complex unity a new sensibility to poverty and to the duties of assistance, new forms of reaction to the economic problems of unemployment and idleness, a new ethic of work . . . within the authoritarian forms of constraint."[69]

The powerful images of lepers and the "ships of fools" that appear in *Madness and Civilisation* have their parallels in the discourses of international relations, too. When the figure of the "madman" replaces that of the leper, what Foucault argues is that "with an altogether new meaning and in a very different culture, the forms would remain—essentially that major form of rigorous division which is social exclusion but spiritual reintegration."[70] The compelling appeal of victims of humanitarian disaster, genocide, or famine reflects "renewed rites of purification and exclusion"[71] and a continuing concern, restated in a new historical formation, with death, order, and meaning.

POWER RELATIONS

We have seen in the discussion of the prison the way processes of the production of knowledge (criminology) and the production of the subject (the delinquent) operate together. These same (disciplinary) practices produce power relations. In this section, I examine Foucault's concept of power in more general terms, looking at power/knowledge in relation to discourse and exploring Foucault's notions of disciplinary power and governmentality.

Relations of power are often seen as repressive. For Foucault, how-ever, they do not just prohibit, they are productive: "We must cease once and for all to describe the effects of power in negative terms: it 'excludes,' it 'represses,' it 'censors,' it 'abstracts,' it 'conceals.' In fact, power pro-duces; it produces reality; it produces domains of objects and rituals of truth."[72] An example is the production of the "individual" through disci-plinary power: "The individual is no doubt the fictitious atom of an 'ideo-logical' representation of society; but he is also a reality fabricated by this specific technology of power that I have called 'discipline.'"[73]

Power relations are not external or superstructural in respect to other relations (economic, knowledge, and so on). On the contrary, power and knowledge are mutually constituted. There are no relations of power with-out corresponding knowledges:

> Power produces knowledge (and not simply by encouraging it because it serves power or by applying it because it is useful). . . . power and knowledge directly imply one another. . . . There is no power relation without the correlative constitution of a field of knowledge, nor any knowledge that does not presuppose and constitute at the same time power relations. These "power-knowledge relations" are to be analysed, therefore, not on the basis of a subject of knowledge who is or is not free in relation to the power system, but, on the contrary, the subject who knows, the object to be known and the modalities must be regarded as so many effects of these fundamental implications of power-knowledge and their historical transformations.[74]

Power is not something that is held on to or possessed. It is not cen-tralized but is exercised from many points. Foucault proposes that an analysis made in terms of power "must not assume that the sovereignty of the state, the form of law, or the overall unity of a domination are given at the outset; rather these are only the terminal forms power takes."[75] Power is omnipresent because "it is produced from one moment to the next, at every point, or rather in every relation from one point to another."[76] It does not emanate from some central point: "Power is everywhere; not because it embraces everything, but because it comes from everywhere."[77]

In the analysis of power relations, the question to be addressed is:

> In a specific type of discourse . . . in a specific form of extortion of truth, appearing historically and in specific places . . . what were the most im-mediate, the most local power relations at work? How did they make pos-sible [particular] kinds of discourses, and conversely, how were these dis-courses used to support power relations? How was the action of these power relations modified by their very exercise . . . with effects of resis-tance, so that there never existed one type of stable subjugation, given once and for all? How were these power relations linked to one another according to the logic of a great strategy?[78]

This view challenges approaches that see a static distribution of power centrally held. For Foucault, any major domination is a hegemonic effect, and there are always points of resistance.[79]

In the study of discourse, this means that specific discourses are not dominant or dominated: "We must not imagine a world of discourse divided between accepted discourse and excluded discourse or between the dominant discourse and the dominated one; but as a multiplicity of discursive elements that can come into play in various strategies."[80] It is a question of analyzing the specific historical relations of power and the discursive practices that sustain or resist them:

> Discourses are not once and for all subservient to power or raised up against it, any more than silences are. . . . Discourse transmits and produces power; it reinforces it, but also undermines and exposes it, renders it fragile and makes it possible to thwart it. In like manner, silence and secrecy are a shelter for power, anchoring its prohibitions; but they also loosen its holds and provide for relatively obscure areas of tolerance.[81]

Foucault gives the example of homosexuality. At one time it was not spoken of. When it became spoken, as part of the imposition of social controls, this also provided the possibility for homosexuality to begin to speak on its own behalf:

> There is not on the one side, a discourse of power, and opposite it, another discourse that runs counter to it. Discourses are tactical elements or blocks operating in the field of force relations; there can exist different and even contradictory discourses within the same strategy; they can, on the contrary, circulate without changing their form from one strategy to another, opposing strategy.[82]

In a given historical culture, particular forms of power will predominate. In France in the seventeenth century, the sovereign right to take life or to let live was replaced by a power to administer life. Foucault characterizes sovereign power by "the right to decide life and death. . . . It was not an absolute privilege: it was conditioned by the defence of the sovereign."[83] The new form of power that came into being, a power over life, evolved in two basic forms: an anatomopolitics of the human body (disciplines) and a biopolitics of the population (regulatory controls). I have considered Foucault's notion of anatomo-politics in the discussion of prisons and disciplinary practices. The concept of biopolitics is developed in his work on governmentality and pastoral power.[84]

These forms of power were vital to the development of capitalism.[85] Foucault refers to Max Weber's work on the "role of an ascetic morality in the first formation of capitalism" but identifies as a new factor, with perhaps a greater impact, "the entry of life into history, that is, the entry of phenomena peculiar to the life of the human species into the order of knowledge and power, into the sphere of political techniques."[86]

Of course the biological had had an impact on the historical for thousands of years: Famines and epidemics are obvious examples. It was a relationship dominated by the threat of death. But, the period of this threat had come to an end in France at least, according to Foucault, with improvements in agricultural production. Gradually, as techniques averted some of the risks, they also came to assume, through knowledge and power, control over "life processes." Part of the biological facts of life passed into the control of knowledge and the political:

> It is not that life has been totally integrated into techniques that govern and administer it; it constantly escapes them. Outside the Western world, famine exists, on a greater scale than ever; and the biological risks confronting the species are perhaps greater and certainly more serious than before the birth of microbiology. But what might be called a society's "threshold of modernity" has been reached when the life of the species is wagered on its own political strategies.[87]

This change can also be characterized as a move from a "symbolics of blood" to an "analytics of sexuality."[88] The change is to a mechanism of power at the overlap of the "body" and "population"; this power is "organised around the management of life rather than the menace of death."[89] For some societies, the blood relation is significant in relations of power. It is part of the manifestations of power and the rituals of power in societies where "the system of alliance, the political form of the sovereign, the differentiation into orders and castes, and the value of descent lines were predominant . . . a society in which famine, epidemics, and violence made death imminent."[90] In such societies "blood constituted one of the fundamental values. . . . Power spoke through blood: the honour of war, the fear of famine, the triumph of death, the sovereign with his sword, executioners and tortures; blood was a reality with a symbolic function."[91] In contrast, societies such as those in contemporary France are societies where "sex" or "sexuality" has replaced "blood" or "sanguinity" as a focus for the mechanisms of power: "The mechanisms of power are addressed to the body, to life, to what causes it to proliferate, to what reinforces the species, its stamina, its ability to dominate, or its capacity for being used."[92]

What Foucault is describing here are two "régimes of power"—these are not distinct, essentialized, or causal. "It is not the soul of two civilisations or the organising principle of two cultural forms that I am attempting to express,"[93] but "régimes of power." There are overlaps and echoes: The modern form of racism can be seen as a haunting of the concern with blood, for example.

THE ETHICAL SUBJECT

Foucault's third axis (or domain of genealogy) constitutes "a historical ontology in relation to ethics through which we constitute ourselves as moral agents."[94] This study, published in the *History of Sexuality,*[95] particularly volumes two and three, involves an investigation of "problems or themes about the self, the ethics of the self, technology of the self"[96] in the pagan world of ancient Greece, and an examination of how these became Christian ethics. The Greeks were concerned not so much with life after death or religion as with their relations to others and to themselves. It was these problems that formed the basis of what they considered to be ethics. Foucault was also struck with two other differences: the way ethics in that period was not related to social or legal institutions that imposed an ethical framework and the concern with an "ethics which was an aesthetics of existence."[97]

Contemporary problems are similar to those of the pagan world and contrast with those of the intervening period of Christian ethics in its various forms. In modern Western societies, there is no longer a widespread belief in a religious foundation for ethics, nor do we accept the intervention of legal mechanisms in what we see as a separate moral or personal sphere. This is particularly problematic for political movements: "Recent liberation movements suffer from the fact that they cannot find any principle on which to base the elaboration of a new ethics. They need an ethics, but they cannot find any other ethics than an ethics founded on so-called scientific knowledge of what the self is, what desire is, what the unconscious is, and so on."[98]

Although this is similar to the problem the Greeks faced, Foucault is not suggesting that this provides us with a solution: He emphasizes that he is not in any way proposing a return to Greek ethics as an "alternative." For Foucault, "there is no exemplary value in a period which is not our period." What this serves to show, however, is that what is "ethical" at any particular moment is not governed by human nature or anthropology. It is not a necessary but rather a historically contingent occurrence that for contemporary ethics desire and pleasure are disconnected, with desire taking priority: This historical contingency is demonstrated by the way that for the Greeks the two were very strongly connected.

What Foucault is thus concerned with is analyzing how, at a particular historical moment, certain things came to be considered as having to do with "ethics." In examining the "history of morals," Foucault distinguishes three elements: people's acts or behavior, the moral code or prescriptions that are imposed, and the kind of relationship you ought to have with yourself, "*rapport à soi,*" which he calls "ethics":[99] "In what we call morals, there is the effective behaviour of people, there are the codes, and there is this kind of relationship to oneself."[100]

The relationship to oneself can be analyzed under four different headings: the ethical substance, the mode of subjection, the self-forming activity or asceticism, and the telos. The first aspect is concerned with the question, "Which is the aspect or part of myself or my behaviour which is concerned with moral conduct?"[101] It is not always the same aspect that is regarded as significant ethically: For contemporary society, feelings are the main field of morality whereas for Christian morality, desire was uppermost. The second aspect, the mode of subjection, is "the way in which people are invited or incited to recognise their moral obligations."[102] Examples here are through divine law (as revealed, for example, in religious texts), through natural law, or through rationality and the claim to universality. The third aspect of the relationship to the self addresses the question, "What are the means by which we can change ourselves in order to become ethical subjects?"[103] Finally, the fourth aspect is the aim, or telos, of moral activity: "Which is the kind of being to which we aspire when we behave in a moral way? For instance, shall we become pure, or immortal, or free, or masters of ourselves, and so on?"[104]

What is distinct at different historical moments is not so much the codes themselves (though these may alter) as the *relationship to oneself* through which the codes are articulated. In other words, what changes is not the moral code but what Foucault has called the "ethics."

This work on ethics is directly linked with Foucault's political activism, through notions of the ethicopolitical. As we have seen, questioning the foundations for ethics leads to problems for contemporary political and social movements and raises some of the same issues as questioning the autonomous, essentialist subject:[105] Again, Foucault is not suggesting that we look to the Greeks for a solution; he is merely underscoring the similarity of the problem. His point is that "everything is dangerous. . . . The ethical political choice we have to make every day is to determine which is the main danger."[106] His political position, then, is one of activism, but an activism that sees not an ultimate solution but a need for recurring, never ending, and ever vigilant political involvement.

CONCLUSION

We have seen that Foucault is concerned to analyze "the complex and unstable process whereby discourse can be both an instrument and an effect of power, but also a hindrance, a stumbling-block, a point of resistance and a starting point for an opposing strategy."[107] Discourse is, in this view, an intensely political practice and one through which "subjects" are produced. We have seen that Foucault examines discursive practices in themselves, separate from their connections with other social practices, in his work on the medical and human sciences as sciences—practices that produce the subject as a subject of knowledge. He also explores the power axis more directly, looking at practices which produce subjects through processes of division and objecticization. He isolates two forms of power: anatomo-power, which operates through disciplinary practices, and biopower, linked with notions of governmentality.

The connection between the subject and "knowledge" through power that Foucault so strongly makes is a central issue for theories of ideology (at least as more recently understood), as suggested in Chapter 2. Foucault himself rejects the notion of "ideology" for several reasons.[108] First, he sees ideology as implying the existence of its virtual opposite, truth. According to Foucault, effects of truth are produced within discourses that are themselves neither true nor false. Second, the concept of ideology requires a subject: For Foucault the subject is not a given; it is produced. The process of subjectification, the production of subjects by practices and techniques, does not require the mediation of the subject's consciousness. Finally, ideology stands in a secondary position to something else that functions as its infrastructure, as its material, economic determinant. Foucault sees knowledge and power as indivisible; the distinction between base and superstructure is not helpful.

What are important for Foucault are the mechanisms for the production of truth, the "games of truth":

> "Truth" is linked in a circular relation with systems of power which produce and sustain it, and to effects of power which it induces and which extend it. A "régime" of truth. . . .
>
> The problem is not changing people's consciousness—or what's in their heads—but the political, economic, institutional régime for the production of truth. . . .
>
> The political question, to sum up, is not error, illusion, alienated consciousness or ideology; it is truth itself.[109]

I do not dispute the points in this rejection. I have argued above that the problematization of the notion of the subject is central to any repoliticization and needs to be considered alongside the problem of ideology. The questions of "truth" and "knowledge" that Foucault explores when he discusses "régimes of truth" are parallel to the concerns of many contemporary writers on ideology, as we shall see particularly in Chapter 5 on Žižek. Most important for the present discussion, Foucault's argument renders untenable any view of knowledge or truth as separate from or having nothing to do with the political. Knowledge itself is repoliticized.

This repoliticization takes place in part through a challenge to the framework that regards truth as having grounds outside the political; this proceeds through an analysis of particular discursive formations that points to their shifting, historical, contingent, and political character. Each of Foucault's substantive books takes a specific area of discourse as its object of study. But the aim in every case is to interrupt *actualité* (the present) and to make it impossible to continue the same depoliticized discourse in the future. For Foucault, "all discourse must be rendered intolerable," as discourse is always a question of the production or legitimation of power, and all power (though inevitable and necessary) is ultimately illegitimate.[110] Discourse serves to conceal, to cover up, that illegitimacy. As we shall see in Chapter 5, Žižek regards the aim of what he calls the "critical intellectual" in a very similar light. According to Žižek:

> The duty of the critical intellectual . . . is precisely *to occupy all the time,* even when the new order . . . stabilizes itself and again renders invisible the hole as such, *the place of this hole,* i.e., to maintain a distance toward every reigning Master-Signifier. The aim is precisely to "produce" the Master Signifier, that is to say, to render visible its "produced," artificial, contingent character.[111]

As we shall see, "social reality" as such requires an organizing "master signifier," or, in Foucauldian terms, "discourse" as such produces an organizing "legitimation of power." The critique of ideology tries to make it impossible to conceal this and to "naturalise" or depoliticize the social structure. In this way, *actualité* is interrupted, continuation of the discourse is rendered problematic, and the promise of repoliticization becomes possible.

For Foucault, resistance is implicit in all relations of power; the political in that sense cannot be extinguished, and the subject remains "free." For Derrida, in a homologous way, deconstruction happens: the discursive practices of logocentrism contain within themselves their own instability, their own points of resistance. Despite the resistance implicit in discursive and disciplinary practices, however, it is through these practices, and most of all, perhaps, through techniques of self-subjectification, that power is translated into technology. Relations of power, subject to processes of legitimization, become a program that is applied by experts and justified by a régime of truth: Truth replaces legitimacy as technologization replaces the political.

NOTES

1. By Hubert L. Dreyfus and Paul Rabinow, in *Michel Foucault: Beyond Structuralism and Hermeneutics, with an Afterword by Michel Foucault* (Hemel Hempstead, UK: Harvester, 1982), for example.

2. The distinction is made by a number of commentators, most influentially perhaps Dreyfus and Rabinow. Rabinow's edited collection embodies this position: Paul Rabinow, ed., *The Foucault Reader* (New York: Random House, 1984). Alan Sheridan argues that the theme of power was implicit in the earlier books, and there is certainly no "reversal": Alan Sheridan, *Michel Foucault: The Will to Truth* (London: Tavistock, 1980). Gilles Deleuze also notes the shift, but again not in terms of a contradiction or a reversal; Gilles Deleuze, *Foucault*, trans. Seán Hand (London: Athlone Press, 1988), 31.

3. Michel Foucault, *The Order of Things: An Archaeology of the Human Sciences* (London: Tavistock, 1970); Michel Foucault, *The Birth of the Clinic: An Archaeology of Medical Perception*, trans. A. M. Sheridan (London: Tavistock, 1973). Archaeology as a method is discussed in Michel Foucault, *The Archaeology of Knowledge*, trans. A. M. Sheridan Smith (London: Routledge, 1989).

4. Michel Foucault, *Discipline and Punish: The Birth of the Prison,* trans. Alan Sheridan (Harmondsworth, UK: Penguin, 1991).

5. Michel Foucault, *Madness and Civilisation: A History of Insanity in the Age of Reason,* trans. Richard Howard (London: Routledge, 1989); Michel Foucault, *The History of Sexuality,* vol. 1: *An Introduction,* trans. Robert Hurley (Harmondsworth, UK: Penguin, 1990); vol. 2: *The Use of Pleasure;* trans. Robert Hurley (Harmondsworth, UK: Penguin, 1992); vol. 3: *The Care of the Self,* trans. Robert Hurley (Harmondsworth, UK: Penguin, 1990).

6. Michel Foucault, "The Order of Discourse," in *Language and Politics,* ed. Michael J. Shapiro, trans. Ian McLeod (Oxford: Blackwell, 1984), 108–138.

7. Michel Foucault, "Nietzsche, Genealogy, History," in *Language, Countermemory, Practice: Selected Essays and Interviews,* ed. Donald F. Bouchard, trans. Donald F. Bouchard and Sherry Simon (Ithaca, NY: Cornell University Press, 1977), 139–164. Also reprinted in Rabinow, *Foucault Reader,* 116.

8. Sheridan, *Will to Truth,* 116.

9. Michel Foucault, "The Subject and Power," in Dreyfus and Rabinow, *Foucault: Beyond Structuralism,* 208. Foucault also calls this "objectivation."

10. Ibid.

11. Ibid.

12. Ibid.

13. Michel Foucault, "On Genealogy of Ethics: An Overview of Work in Progress," in Rainbow, *The Foucault Reader,* 351. This is the edited version; the full original first appeared as "Afterword (1983)" in *Michel Foucault: Beyond Structuralism and Hermeneutics,* ed. Hubert L. Dreyfus and Paul Rabinow, 2nd ed. (Chicago: University of Chicago Press, 1983), 229–252.

Deleuze's analysis of Foucault's work involves a similar threefold structure using the dimensions of knowledge, power, and the self (Deleuze, *Foucault*). He draws our attention to Foucault's additional elaborations of the dimension of power. In the case of modern disciplinary societies, the practice of power has two functions: anatomopolitics and biopolitics (Foucault, *History of Sexuality,* vol. 1, 139). This is a useful distinction. Anatomopolitics is the imposition of particular taste or conduct on a small, confined multiplicity—a particular body. Biopolitics, in contrast, is administering or controlling life in a large, open multiplicity—a particular population.

Foucault uses the term "ethics" in a very specific way. He distinguishes "ethics" from a moral code and describes it as "the kind of relationship you ought to have with yourself . . . and which determines how the individual is supposed to constitute himself as the moral subject of his own actions" (Foucault, "Genealogy of Ethics," 352).

14. Foucault, *Use of Pleasure,* 6.

15. Ibid.

16. Ibid.

17. Ibid., 6–7.

18. Ibid., 11–12.

19. Ibid.

20. Ibid.

21. Slavoj Žižek, *The Sublime Object of Ideology* (London: Verso, 1989), 89–107.

22. Michel Foucault, *Madness and Civilisation.*

23. The work of Žižek, discussed in detail in Chapter 6, is exemplary here.

24. Foucault, *Order of Things,* 387.

25. Ibid., xxiv.

26. Michel Foucault, "Politics and the Study of Discourse," in *The Foucault Effect: Studies in Governmentality, with Two Lectures by and an Interview with Michel Foucault,* ed. Graham Burchell, Colin Gordon, and Peter Miller (London: Harvester Wheatsheaf, 1991), 63.

27. Ibid.

28. Foucault, *Archaeology of Knowledge,* 27.

29. Ibid.

30. Foucault, *Order of Things,* xiii.

31. See also the discussion of "naming" in Chapter 5.

32. Foucault, *Archaeology of Knowledge,* 5.

33. Ibid., 23.

34. Ibid., 47–48.

35. Foucault, "Nietzsche, Genealogy, History," 140.

36. Ibid., 142.

37. Ibid.

38. Ibid., 143.

39. Foucault, *Archaeology of Knowledge,* 49.

40. Ibid.

41. Ernesto Laclau and Chantal Mouffe, *Hegemony and Socialist Strategy: Towards a Radical Democratic Politics* (London: Verso, 1985), 145, no. 13.

42. Foucault, "Politics and the Study of Discourse," 58.

43. Ibid., 59.

44. For an extensive discussion of "materiality" in Foucault, see Judith Butler, *Bodies That Matter: On the Discursive Limits of 'Sex'* (London: Routledge, 1993).

45. Foucault, "Politics and the Study of Discourse," 60–61.

46. Ibid., 67.

47. In Freud's description the role of dream work is similar in that it does not determine the content but the *form* of dreams. See Chapter 2.

48. Foucault, "Politics and the Study of Discourse," 69.

49. Michel Foucault, "Intellectuals and Power: A Conversation Between Michel Foucault and Gilles Deleuze," in Bouchard, *Language, Counter-memory, Practice,* 208.

50. Foucault, *Discipline and Punish,* 231.

51. Ibid., 232.

52. Ibid., 233.

53. Ibid. The process of reform of prisoners gives what Foucault calls the "carceral machinery" its autonomy from the judicial process. Because the prison is required to produce this transformation in individuals, to render them docile and useful, and because this involves "techniques of a disciplinary type,"

the prison becomes largely independent from and not answerable to any other authority.

54. Jenny Edkins, *Famines and Modernity: Pictures of Hunger, Concepts of Famine, Practices of Aid* (Minneapolis: University of Minnesota Press, forthcoming).

55. Foucault, *Discipline and Punish*, 249.

56. Ibid.

57. Ibid., 251.

58. Ibid.

59. Ibid.

60. Ibid., 255.

61. Ibid., 256.

62. Foucault, *Discipline and Punish*, 272.

63. Ibid.

64. Ibid., 277.

65. Ibid., 304.

66. Ibid., 305.

67. Ibid., 138.

68. Ibid., 167.

69. Foucault, *Madness and Civilisation*, 46.

70. Ibid., 7.

71. Ibid., 3.

72. Foucault, *Discipline and Punish*, 194.

73. Ibid.

74. Ibid., 27–28.

75. Foucault, *History of Sexuality*, vol. 1, 92.

76. Ibid.

77. Ibid., 93.

78. Ibid., 97.

79. For a further discussion of resistance and what this implies for notions of freedom, see, for example, Jeremy Moss, ed., *The Later Foucault: Politics and Philosophy* (London: Sage, 1998).

80. Foucault, *History of Sexuality*, vol. 1, 100.

81. Ibid., 101.

82. Ibid., 101–102.

83. Ibid., 135–136.

84. Burchell, Gordon, and Miller, *The Foucault Effect*.

85. Ibid., 141.

86. Ibid., 141–142.

87. Ibid., 143.

88. Ibid., 149.

89. Ibid., 147.

90. Ibid.

91. Ibid.

92. Ibid.

93. Ibid., 148.

94. Foucault, "Genealogy of Ethics," 351.

95. Foucault, *The History of Sexuality*, vol. 1; *The Use of Pleasure*; *The Care of the Self*. See also Michel Foucault, "Technologies of the Self," in *Technologies of the Self*, ed. Luther H. Martin, Huck Gutman, and Patrick H. Hutton (Amherst: University of Massachusetts Press, 1988), 16–49.

96. Foucault, "Genealogy of Ethics," 342.

97. Foucault, "Genealogy of Ethics," 343.

98. Ibid.

99. Ibid., 352.

100. Ibid., 355.

101. Ibid., 352.

102. Ibid., 353.

103. Ibid., 354.

104. Ibid., 355.

105. I consider these in Chapter 2 and discuss them further in the next chapter, when I examine the political consequences of deconstruction.

106. Foucault, "Genealogy of Ethics," 343.

107. Foucault, *History of Sexuality,* vol. 1, 101.

108. Michel Foucault, *Power/Knowledge: Selected Interviews and Other Writings, 1972–1977,* ed. Colin Gordon, trans. Colin Gordon, Leo Marshall, John Mepham, and Kate Soper (Brighton, UK: Harvester, 1980), 118–119.

109. Ibid., 133.

110. François Ewald, presentation at the Foucault Anniversary Conference, organized by Signs of the Times, London, June 25, 1994.

111. Slavoj Žižek, *Tarrying with the Negative: Kant, Hegel and the Critique of Ideology* (Durham, NC: Duke University Press, 1993), 2.

4

Derrida and the Force of Law

Deconstruction, Jacques Derrida notes, is generally practiced in two ways or styles: The first "takes on the demonstrative and apparently ahistorical allure of logico-formal paradoxes. The other, more historical or more anamnesic, seems to proceed through readings of texts, meticulous interpretations and genealogies."[1] Much of Derrida's work comprises these detailed readings of texts, often of other philosophers—Plato, Emmanuel Levinas, Edmund Husserl—or writers in social and political theory—Lévi-Strauss, Freud, Jean-Jacques Rousseau, and more recently, Marx. The discussion of deconstruction in this chapter looks at both practices and points to strong resonances between Derrida's work and that of Foucault and Žižek. It is based on a reading and cross-reading in relation to ideology and the subject. This goes against the grain of much commentary, which is often more concerned to draw boundaries and make distinctions.

It is worth emphasizing at the start that I argue for a reading of Derrida that sees his work as addressing "the political" from the first. His initial critique of binary oppositions stresses the violent hierarchy they impose. His work on the undecidable is central to the argument concerning repoliticization developed here. The chapter begins with an introductory overview of Derrida's work on the metaphysics of presence; this is followed by an examination of deconstructive approaches and notions of the force of law in relation to issues of depoliticization and technologization as we have encountered them thus far. The first part of the chapter gives a review of some of the main notions used in Derrida's work: "logocentrism," "presence," *différance*, "supplementarity," the "constitutive outside," and "deconstruction." The next part parallels the discussion of Foucault's work on the prison in Chapter 3. First I look at what the notion of deconstruction involves. Then I give a brief exposition of part of Derrida's essay "Signature Event Context," which serves as a demonstration of "deconstruction" in the Derridean manner.[2] Second, I discuss the concepts of

65

"authority" and "force" in Derrida's more recent work. I examine the relationship between *logos* and force and its bearing on notions of technologization and depoliticization.

LOGOCENTRISM AND *DIFFÉRANCE*

Derrida's critique of Western metaphysics, in which he follows Friedrich Nietzsche and Martin Heidegger, begins with the observation that Western thought is structured in binary terms: spoken/written; good/evil; absence/presence; man/woman; identity/difference. These are not opposites for Derrida; what is significant for him is that they are hierarchical, with one of the pair being valued more highly and privileged over the other: The opposition produces the terms *along with* their relationship. In *Writing and Difference*, Derrida focuses on the privileging of the spoken over the written word.[3] The spoken is assumed in Western metaphysics to be somehow immediate and hence transparent. In Barbara Johnson's words:

> Whether or not perfect understanding always occurs *in fact* this image of perfectly self-present meaning is . . . the underlying ideal of Western culture. Derrida has termed this belief in the self-presentation of meaning "Logocentrism," from the Greek word *Logos* (meaning speech, logic, reason, the Word of God). Writing, on the other hand, is considered by the logocentric system to be only a representation of speech, a secondary substitute designed for use only when speaking is impossible. Writing is thus a second-rate activity that tries to overcome distance.[4]

So for Derrida "logocentrism" is "the metaphysics of phonetic writing (for example, of the alphabet) which was fundamentally . . . nothing but the most original and powerful ethnocentrism, in the process of imposing itself on the world, controlling in one and the same order: 1. the concept of writing . . . 2. the history of metaphysics . . . 3. the concept of science."[5]

The rejection of writing is the move by which philosophy constitutes itself as unaffected by the contingency of the written word. The privileging of voice becomes the founding moment of the metaphysics of presence. According to Jonathan Culler in his introduction to Derrida's work, this "phonocentrism" is inextricably associated with the logocentrism Derrida sees in philosophy. This is "the 'logocentrism' of metaphysics, the orientation of philosophy toward an order of meaning—thought, truth, reason, logic, the Word—conceived as existing in itself, as foundation."[6] Logocentrism is bound up with the notion of being as presence and a "metaphysics of presence," that is, a metaphysics that seeks for foundations, origins, in a series of "present" poles in oppositions. Each of the "privileged" concepts involves a notion of presence and is treated as a centering, grounding force: "In oppositions . . . the superior term belongs to the logos and is a higher presence; the inferior term marks a fall. Logocentrism thus assumes the priority of the first term and conceives the second in relation to it, as a complication, a negation, a manifestation, or a disruption of the first."[7] In any analysis, for example, it is accepted procedure to start with the "normal" case and deal later with exceptions, aberrations, and so forth.

The value of "presence" is embedded in our thinking—"showing"; "revealing"; "making clear." When viewed from within the metaphysics of presence, writing *represents* speech, which itself *represents* thought: It is "representing a representer, supplement of a supplement." In the political order, Rousseau's critique of representation is based on how it involves this supplanting or supplementing of presence: "The moment the people is legitimately assembled as a sovereign body, the jurisdiction of the government wholly lapses, the executive power is suspended. . . . For in the presence of the person represented, representatives no longer exist."[8] Thus the presence of "live" audiences or demonstrations such as those seen in Europe in 1989 pose a challenge to the notion of representation: "Praise of the assembled people at the festival or at the political forum is always a critique of representation. The legitimising instance, in the city as in language—speech or writing—and the arts, is the representer present in person: source of legitimacy and sacred origin."[9] This is a challenge to the authority invested in political institutions. But this critique involves a notion of first presence, which is problematic for Derrida. What we have is an "indefinite cycle: represented source of representation, the origin of the image can in turn represent its representers, replace its substitutes, supply its supplements. Folded, returning to itself, representing itself, sovereign, presence is then—and barely—only the supplement of a supplement."[10]

An example that demonstrates some of the problems with the logocentric notion of presence is the "presence" of motion in an arrow in flight. At the present moment, an arrow is clearly still—and yet it *is* in motion. This "presence of motion" is conceivable only if every instant is conceived of as already marked in some way with "traces" of the past and the future. This paradox of the "absence of the present" recalls work from early twentieth-century physics that addresses similar problems. Werner Heisenberg's uncertainty principle, for instance, wave/particle duality, and the problem of simultaneity, discussed in the special theory of relativity, are all dealing with the challenge to notions of time and cause in Newtonian physics. They also challenge the classical notions of objects. The mathematics of quantum mechanics tackles the difficulty of conceptualizing and working with these "impossible" formulations.[11] For Derrida, these problems of the "present" are also bound up with problems of the "real." The notion of the real as what is present leads to the paradox of motion: "If motion is to be present, presence must already be marked by difference and deferral. . . . The notion of the present is derived: an effect of differences."[12]

This leads to Derrida's introduction of *différance* as an alternative to the metaphysics of presence: "Thus one comes to posit presence—and specifically consciousness, the Being beside itself of consciousness—no longer as the absolutely central form of being but rather as a 'determination' and as an 'effect.' A determination or an effect within a system which is no longer that of presence but of *différance*."[13] This is an example of "deconstruction" (which I discuss in more detail below): The hierarchy between presence and absence is inverted and displaced. In the opposition presence/absence, "a deconstruction would involve the demonstration that for presence to function as it is said to, it must have the qualities that supposedly belong to its opposite, absence. Thus, instead of defining absence in terms of presence, as *its* negative, we can treat 'presence' as the effect of a generalized absence, or . . . of *différance*."[14] For example, when a word is spoken, the noise that is "present" is inhabited by traces of words, of forms, that are not spoken. It works, as a signifier, *only because of* those traces: "What is supposedly present is already complex and differential, marked by difference, a product of differences."[15]

The notion of *différance* is Derrida's attempt to show how two opposing terms function within thought. The opposition relies on an illusion. Saussure has already shown, as we saw in Chapter 2, how language is a system of differences rather than a collection of meaningful terms that pre-exist language. Meaning, as Saussure shows and Derrida elaborates, relies on "difference." But there are two aspects to this in the production of meaning, and Derrida's term incorporates both. "As soon as there is meaning there is difference. Derrida's word for this lag inherent in any signifying act is *différance,* from the French verb *différer,* which means both 'to differ' and 'to defer.' What Derrida attempts to demonstrate is that this *différance* inhabits the very core of what appears to be immediate and present."[16]

We can see the way Derrida's term *différance* includes notions of difference and deferral at work in the example of the unconscious in Freud. This is parallel to the Lacanian account of the subject (elaborated further in Chapter 5): The notion of deferral has obvious resonances with Lacan's *point de capiton,* where signification retroactively becomes what it already was.[17] Freud's investigations deconstruct oppositions by identifying what is at stake in our attempts to repress the undesirable second term. He shows that understanding the second term can be a condition of understanding the first. The most general example, of course, is in the notion of the subject and the conscious/unconscious. Freud's work deconstructs the definition of the Cartesian subject in terms of consciousness by showing the unconscious as prior, embracing the conscious.[18] This could be seen as making the unconscious into some form of repressed, hidden conscious, ready to be revealed or discovered in psychoanalysis.

Freud, however, distinguishes between the unconscious and the preconscious, whose memories *can* be recovered. As discussed in Chapter 2, the unconscious is inaccessible to consciousness, and moreover, it is both constituted or produced *by* repression and at the same time is *the agent of* repression: "Like *différance*, which designates the impossible origin of difference in differing and of differing in difference, the unconscious is a nonoriginary origin, which Freud calls primary repression."[19] In other words, the unconscious is both the agent that begins the first repression and that which is constituted by repression: "If the discovery of the unconscious is a demonstration that nothing in the human subject is ever simple, that thoughts and desires are already doubled and divided, it turns out that the unconscious itself is not a simple hidden reality but always, in Freud's speculations, a complex and differential product."[20]

As Derrida puts it:

> The unconscious is not, as we know, a hidden, virtual, or potential self-presence. It differs from, and defers, itself; which doubtless means that it is woven of differences, and also that it sends out delegates, representatives, proxies; but without any chance that the giver of proxies could "exist," might be present, be "itself" somewhere, and with even less chance that it might become conscious. In this sense . . . the "unconscious" is no more a "thing" than it is any other thing, is no more a thing than it is a virtual or masked consciousness. This radical alterity as concerns every possible mode of presence is marked by the irreducibility of the after-effect, the delay. . . . The alterity of the "unconscious" makes us concerned not with horizons of modified—past or future—presents, but with a "past" that has never been present, and which never will be, whose future to come will never be a *production* or a reproduction in the form of presence.[21]

Freud finds in his case studies that the determining event in a neurosis frequently *never happens* as such but is constructed afterward by some sort of a textual mechanism in the unconscious. In this "deferred action," the scene often only becomes what it is *afterward:* "The irreducibility of the 'effect of deferral'—such, no doubt is Freud's discovery."[22]

Derrida elaborates this further, stressing the role of the trace and the supplement:

> The unconscious text is already a weave of pure traces, differences in which meaning and force are united—a text nowhere present, consisting of archives which are *always already* transcriptions. Originary prints. Everything begins with reproduction. Always already: repositories of a meaning which was never present, whose signified presence is always reconstituted by deferral, *nachträglich,* belatedly, supplementarily: for *nachträglich* also means supplementary. The call of the supplement is primary, here, and it hollows out that which will be reconstituted by deferral as the present.[23]

THE LOGIC OF THE SUPPLEMENT

The "supplement" is an example of what Derrida calls "undecidables": "unities of simulacrum, 'false' verbal properties (nominal or semantic) that can no longer be included within philosophical (binary) opposition, but which, however, inhabit philosophical opposition, resisting and disorganizing it, *without ever* constituting a third term, without ever leaving room for a solution in the form of speculative dialectics."[24] I reexamine the notion of undecidables later in the chapter, when I analyze Derrida's argument concerning the "force of law" and justice; the undecidable is central to the discussion of depoliticization and the political, as I noted in Chapter 1. Undecidables are terms that follow a particular "logic," different from that of logocentrism. They contain *within themselves* an ambiguity, a duplicity of meaning. They are *neither* one thing *nor* the other, and at the same time they are simultaneously *both*. Examples are the *pharmakon*, in Plato, which is "neither remedy nor poison, neither good nor evil, neither the inside nor the outside, neither speech nor writing" and the *supplement*, which is "neither a plus nor a minus, neither the outside nor the complement of an inside, neither accident nor essence."[25]

Derrida sees undecidables as marking the "interval" between the overturning of the hierarchy of opposites and the emergence of a new term. Undecidables are terms that embody *différance* within themselves—they resist specification; they incorporate opposites. But they are to be distinguished from Hegelian notions of contradiction: They cannot be resolved. The undecidable "situates . . . the unconscious of philosophical contradiction, the unconscious which ignores contradiction to the extent that [it] belongs to the logic of speech, discourse, consciousness, presence, truth, etc."[26]

The logic of the undecidable can be seen in the "supplement." The "supplement" has two distinct meanings, "an inessential extra, added to something complete in itself, but . . . added in order to complete, to compensate for a lack in what was supposed to be complete in itself."[27] These two meanings of supplement are linked in a powerful logic. Both meanings present the supplement as exterior, foreign to the "essential" nature of that to which it is added or in which it is substituted. It is both inessential and essential: It is the "constitutive outside" discussed by Henry Staten,[28] as we shall see shortly.

This notion of supplementarity leads to the distinction between inside and outside and the idea of a "reality" *itself*. In Derrida's words:

> Through this sequence of supplements a necessity is announced: that of an infinite chain, ineluctably multiplying the supplementary mediations that produce the sense of the very thing they defer: the mirage of the thing itself, of immediate presence, of originary perception. Immediacy is

derived. That all begins with the intermediary is what is indeed "inconceivable [to reason]."[29]

Presence is thus always deferred, and what lies outside the "texts" is more supplements, chains of supplements. This puts into question the distinction between inside and outside. What is called "real life" is "constituted by the logic of supplementarity."[30] So presence is not originary but constituted by absence (a lack), by difference.

The privileging of speech over writing, with writing set aside as supplement, is basic to the whole of Western metaphysics. It is not a choice that could have been avoided, and it can be linked with "the idea of the world, of world-origin, that arises from the difference between the worldly and the non-worldly, the outside and the inside, ideality and non-ideality, universal and non-universal, transcendental and empirical, etc."[31] The moment of one's own speech serves as a reference for these distinctions and also enables one to treat the distinctions as hierarchical oppositions. In other words, the privileging of speech over writing, which is the base of this entire construction, is itself based on "*s'entendre parler,*" which includes the idea of hearing oneself speak and understanding oneself simultaneously. In a sense this replaces the cogito and gives us another notion of the subject—as constituted by a presence that is nothing more than the product of difference and deferral. There is no way out of this, however. "Theories grounded on presence . . . undo themselves as the supposed foundation or ground proves to be the product of . . . difference, differentiation and deferral. But [this] does not lead to a new theory that sets everything straight. . . . There is no reason to believe that a theoretical enterprise could ever free itself from [logocentric] premises."[32]

The discussion of the relation between inside and outside and the role of the supplement is translated by Staten into the notion of the "constitutive outside": the outside as necessary for the constitution of the essence.[33] There is a comparison to be made here with Emile Durkheim's interest in the "boundaries" of the social in defining, or attempting to define, the social itself (hence his interest in deviance, crime, suicide, etc.) and with Foucault's concern with the role of dividing practices in the constitution of the subject. In Derrida's conception of accidents, for example,

If essence is *always* exposed to the possibility of accidents, is it not then a necessary, rather than a chance, possibility, and if it is always and necessarily possible, is it not then an *essential* possibility? . . . Generalising the principle of the accidental, then, we can say that it is the "outside" of essence. . . . Derrida works something like a figure-field switch on this conception and takes the outside to be necessary to the constitution of a phenomenon in its as-such, a condition of the possibility of the inside. . . . In this sense of a "constitutive outside," the outside is not "accidental" as indefinite, since it is necessary for a given kind of as-such; it is accidental as non-essence that befalls essence.[34]

An example is memory. A necessary condition for memory is "forgetfulness"—if memory were complete, it would not be memory but something else.

Discourses are constituted by a number of other complex processes of interweaving and superimposition. Two notions in particular are important here: "iterability" and "graft." Both have resonances with other work on discourse. Iterability is necessary for signification: "Something can be a signifying sequence only if it is iterable, only if it can be repeated in various serious and nonserious contexts, cited and parodied. Imitation is not an accident that befalls an original but its condition of possibility."[35] It also points to the issue of context, which cannot be "saturated"—total context can never be specified: "Meaning is context bound, but context is boundless."[36] Despite the arguments of critics of deconstruction, ultimate indeterminacy (of meaning) need not be a reason for regarding theory as pointless—a great deal of practical science and engineering is based on assumptions of indeterminacy, for example. Nor is there a *choice* between seeking for true meaning or origin and the free play or absolute indeterminacy of meaning.

This leads to the second notion, that of "grafts." Meaning is produced by a process of grafting, related to ideas of articulation and rearticulation in other approaches. Using the notion of "grafts" is to "treat discourse as the product of various sorts of combinations or insertions. Exploring the iterability of language, its ability to function in new contexts with new force, a treatise on textual grafting would attempt to classify various ways of inserting one discourse in another or intervening in the discourse one is interpreting. . . . Deconstruction is . . . an attempt to identify grafts in the texts it analyses. . . . Deconstruction elucidates the heterogeneity of the text."[37] Derrida himself employs techniques of graft—such as relegating something to the margins or retaining old names while grafting a new meaning upon them.

DECONSTRUCTION

Deconstruction begins with the demonstration of philosophy's use of binary oppositions and hierarchy, but it does not stop there, nor does it then try to annul the opposition. If the "opposition" were merely neutralized, this would not work as an intervention. What we are dealing with is not a "peaceful coexistence" but a "violent hierarchy." According to Rodolphe Gasché, the dominant misconception about deconstruction is its "identification . . . with the neutralization or mutual annulment of contradicting concepts or textual strata."[38] This view is, says Gasché, at the base of most use of deconstruction in literary criticism and is known as the theory of self-reflection or self-deconstruction. It relies on a suprahistorical position, where it can speak from an absolute point of view.

In contrast to this view, Derrida's approach itself is historically and politically situated. By Derrida's account,

> On the one hand, we must traverse a phase of *overturning*. . . . To deconstruct an opposition, first of all, is to overturn the hierarchy at a given moment. To overlook this phase of overturning is to forget the conflictual and subordinating structure of opposition. Therefore one might proceed too quickly to a *neutralization* that *in practice* would leave the previous field untouched, leaving one no hold on the previous opposition, thereby preventing any means of *intervening* in the field effectively. We know what always have been the *practical* (particularly *political*) effects of *immediately* jumping *beyond* oppositions, and of protests in the simple form of *neither* this *nor* that.[39]

Derrida's style is an attempt to solve some of these problems. He analyzes texts closely, showing, for example, how "text functions *against* its own explicit (metaphysical) assertions . . . by inscribing a *systematic* 'other message' behind or through what is being said."[40] There is a double procedure, which involves the use of the concepts or premises one is undermining: One must operate within these concepts in order to deconstruct them. The result is a reversal of the hierarchical opposition, which produces a displacement. A deconstruction of the notion of cause, for example, applies it to causation itself and shows that either cause or effect can occupy the position of origin. Origin is then no longer originary; it loses its metaphysical privilege.[41]

This type of deconstructive approach is not looking for meaning in the text, nor is it looking for the relation between text and "reality." For Derrida,

> There is nothing outside of the text [there is no outside-text; *il n'y a pas de hors-texte*]. . . . What we have tried to show . . . is that in what one calls the real life of these existences. . . beyond and behind what one believes can be circumscribed as . . . text, there has never been anything but writing; there has never been anything but supplements, substitutive significations which could only come forth in a chain of differential references, the "real" supervening, and being added only while taking on meaning from a trace and from the invocation of the supplement, etc.[42]

This is crucial. Deconstruction does not offer a way out of the metaphysics of presence: It offers only an analysis of it, and even that in its own terms.

This leads to problems, of course. The criticism that deconstruction is a self-defeating method because it has to speak the language it is trying to critique is difficult to counter. Derrida argues that

> there is no sense in doing without the concepts of metaphysics in order to shake metaphysics. We have no language—no syntax and no lexicon— which is foreign to this history: we can pronounce not a single destructive proposition which has not already had to slip into the form, the logic, and the implicit postulations of precisely what it seeks to contest. . . . Every particular borrowing brings along with it the whole of metaphysics.[43]

It is possible to argue that this is why deconstruction has to operate in the way it does: "If the traditional logic of meaning as an unequivocal structure of mastery *is* Western metaphysics, the deconstruction of metaphysics cannot simply combat logocentric meaning by opposing some other meaning to it. *Différance* is not a 'concept' or 'idea' that is 'truer' than presence. It can only be a process of textual work, a strategy of writing."[44] The approach proceeds by "the careful teasing out [of] the warring forces of signification within the text itself."[45] It is a form of critique. It is not an examination of the flaws or imperfections of the theoretical text but an analysis that seeks to explore the grounds of possibility of the text: "The critique reads back from what seems natural, obvious, self-evident or universal, in order to show that these things have their history, their reasons for being the way they are, their effects on what follows from them, and that the starting point is not a (natural) given but a (cultural) construct, usually blind to itself."[46] The question asked is not, "What does it mean?" but, "What does it presuppose?"

It is this use of metaphysics that allows "intervention." By using concepts from metaphysics, "borrowing" them in order to name what cannot be named within the closure of philosophy, the concepts suffer a mutation, and this permits an intervention within the discourse of philosophy: "The necessity of borrowing one's resources from the logic to be deconstructed is not only no inconvenience or calamity, as some have believed, but is rather the very condition of finding a foothold in the discourse to be deconstructed."[47] Or as Derrida puts it in *Writing and Difference:* "We cannot give up this metaphysical complicity without also giving up the critique we are directing against this complicity."[48]

It is while recognizing these constraints that the deconstructive method Derrida proposes has developed its strategies. Deconstruction proceeds by a "double gesture" or "double science": a phase of reversal and a phase of displacement. The second stage produces concepts unheard of in philosophical discourse, which Gasché has called "infrastructures": "They represent the *surplus* of the conceptual dyads or of the totality of a discourse as well as what prevents them or that totality from achieving closure. They are in other words a *lack*."[49] Culler describes the process as follows: "To deconstruct an opposition is to undo and displace it, to situate it differently."[50] This involves two steps: first, to show that the opposition is a metaphysical and ideological imposition by bringing out its assumptions and its role and by showing how it is undone in texts that rely on it; second, to maintain the opposition by using it in the argument, and then by reinstating it with a reversal that gives it a different status and impact. As we have seen, this method lays deconstruction open to misunderstanding and criticism: "Working in this way, with a double movement, both inside and outside previous categories and distinctions, deconstruction is uncomfortably positioned and particularly open to attack and misunderstanding . . . both as an anarchism . . . and . . . as an accessory to the hierarchies it denounces."[51]

Culler's summary of what is involved in a deconstructive reading is useful here, although he is "risking reductiveness for the sake of explicitness." A deconstructive critique will be on the lookout for different sorts of conflict: value-laden hierarchies where the second term, "treated as a negative, marginal, or supplementary version of the first . . . prove[s] to be the condition of possibility of the first"; and points of condensation, "where a single term brings together different lines of argument or sets of values." It will attempt to subvert the oppositions which are necessary to the text's argument. It will also be looking for other forms of the text's "difference from itself," and by attention to the marginal and reading against the grain try to demonstrate "the return in a displaced or disguised form of a procedure that work claimed to criticise in others . . . [which] fold[s] the text back on itself."[52]

"SIGNATURE EVENT CONTEXT"

An example of how Derrida's deconstruction works and, in particular, how it employs the "outside," or the negative, is his controversial essay on J. L. Austin's speech act theory, "Signature Event Context."[53] It prompted a response from John R. Searle, a rejoinder from Derrida, and further criticism and responses.[54] In the essay Derrida examines the role of "absence" in differentiating writing from other forms of "communication." In the accepted sense, "writing" is regarded as an extended form of communication. Writing is undertaken with the intention of communication of thought: The "thought" exists prior to the communication, and writing is one among other means of communication.[55] Writing extends communication by making it possible to communicate to people who are absent. The notion of absence is important here: Derrida underscores this to return to it later in deconstructing the model. He argues that in fact every sign presupposes a certain "absence" and that this makes it more difficult to use "absence" as specific to writing. If this is so, then a shift occurs, and all the concepts to do with the model of communication as generally followed become questionable. I concentrate here on Derrida's analysis of the performative as opposed to the constative, a distinction Austin used. Derrida demonstrates that contradictions arising through the use of the opposition performative/constative are unavoidable *and* that they deconstruct the categories themselves.

As far as any element of spoken language is concerned, the identity of the signifying form must be recognizable despite variations (in accent, emphasis, etc.): "This unity of the signifying form only constitutes itself by virtue of its iterability, by the possibility of its being repeated in the absence not only of its 'referent' but in the absence of a determinate signified or of the intention of actual signification, as well as of all intention of present communication."[56] The possibility of any mark's being cited, put between quotation marks and thus broken from its context, is another part of what constitutes a mark: It is "the possibility of disengagement and citational graft which belongs to the structure of every mark . . . and which constitutes every mark." These characteristics of a "mark"—citationality, duplication or duplicity, and iterability—are not accidental. Without them, "a mark could not even have the functions called 'normal.' What would a mark be that could not be cited? Or one whose origins would not get lost along the way?"[57] A certain "absence" is thus presupposed by the spoken language.

Austin contrasts the performative utterance with the constative utterance (classical assertions, which can be considered true or false). This introduces a new notion of communication that *includes* the performative, or in other words includes the total situation. The crucial difference for Derrida is that the performative does not *describe* something that exists outside of and prior to language, as it is claimed the constative does. Instead, it produces or transforms *a situation,* and it involves notions of force. This notion of Austin's "has shattered the concept of communication as a purely semiotic, linguistic, or symbolic concept. The performative is a 'communication' which is not limited strictly to the transference of a semantic content that is already constituted and dominated by an orientation toward truth."[58]

Derrida draws attention to the continuing importance Austin gives to the "conscious presence of the intention of the speaking subject,"[59] so that the performative remains the communication of an intentional meaning: The speaker knows what the performative is designed to accomplish. If in some way the performance does *not* have the "desired" effect, it is no longer a performative and Austin regards it as having failed. Derrida sees this as typical of other moves in the Western philosophical tradition:

It consists in recognizing that the possibility of the negative . . . is in fact a structural possibility, that failure is an essential risk of the operations under consideration; then, in a move which is almost *immediately simultaneous,* in the name of a kind of ideal regulation, it excludes that risk as accidental, exterior, one which teaches us nothing about the linguistic phenomenon being considered. This is all the more curious—and, strictly speaking, untenable—in view of Austin's ironic denunciation of the "fetishized" opposition: *value/fact.*[60]

Austin's refusal to follow the consequences is clear. He does not ponder what happens if

a possibility—a possible risk—is *always* possible, and is in some sense a necessary possibility. [Or] whether—once such a necessary possibility of infelicity is recognized—infelicity still constitutes an accident. What is success when the possibility of infelicity continues to constitute its structure?[61]

This same line of approach leads Austin to refuse the possibility of *citation.* He wants to exclude from something he calls "ordinary language" instances when utterances are spoken by an actor on stage, in a soliloquy or a poem. Austin regards these as parasitic, abnormal, and with no place in a theory of the performative utterance.

Again Derrida questions this placing of the risk outside, as the excluded failure. He asks the question:

Is this risk rather its internal and positive condition of possibility? Is that outside its inside, the very force and law of its emergence? . . . What Austin excludes as anomaly, exception, "non-serious," citation . . . is the determined modification of a general citationality—or rather, a general iterability—without which there would not even be a "successful" performative? So that—a paradoxical but unavoidable conclusion—a successful performative is necessarily an "impure" performative.[62]

It is Derrida's contention, and in this he is referring to events in general, that there is a strange logic at work here. What we have is not a distinction between utterances that are "iterable" and those that are not—on the contrary, all performative utterances, to succeed, must inevitably be iterable. The distinction is one between different *kinds* of iterability.

The category of "intention" will retain a place in this schema but will not be part of an opposition between "citational utterances, on the one hand, and singular and original event-utterances on the other." So intention is no longer "through and through present to itself and its content"; the iteration introduces an essential "cleft." Derrida goes on to posit a general graphemic structure to every "communication": "A general iterability . . . constitutes a violation of the allegedly rigorous purity of every event of discourse or every speech act."[63] He concludes: "We are witnessing . . . the increasingly powerful historical expansion of *a general writing,* of which the system of speech, consciousness, meaning, presence, truth, etc., would be only an effect, and should be analyzed as such. It is the exposure of this effect that I have called elsewhere logocentrism."[64]

At the end of the essay on Austin, Derrida summarizes what he has been doing:

> Very schematically: an opposition of metaphysical concepts (e.g. speech/writing, presence/absence, etc.) is never the confrontation of two terms, but a hierarchy and the order of a subordination. Deconstruction cannot be restricted or immediately pass to a neutralization: it must, through a double gesture, a double science, a double writing—put into practice a *reversal* of the classical opposition *and* a general *displacement* of the system. It is on that condition alone that deconstruction will provide the means of *intervening* in the field of oppositions it criticizes and that is also a field of non-discursive forces. Every concept, moreover, belongs to a systematic chain and constitutes in itself a system of predicates. There is no concept that is metaphysical in itself. There is a labor—metaphysical or not—performed on conceptual systems. Deconstruction does not consist in moving from one concept to another, but in reversing and displacing a conceptual order as well as the non-conceptual order with which it is articulated. . . . It is those predicates . . . [that have] always *resisted* the prior organization of forces, always constituted the *residue* irreducible to the dominant force organizing the hierarchy that we may refer to, in brief, as logocentric.[65]

DECONSTRUCTION AND THE POLITICAL

Despite the commentators who regard the deconstructive approach as non-political or "conservative," it is clear from his earliest work that Derrida does not see it this way. On the contrary, he argues:

> [Deconstruction is] a way of taking a position, in its work of analysis, concerning the political and institutional structures that make possible and govern our practices. . . . Deconstruction is neither a methodological reform that should reassure the organization in place nor a flourish of irresponsible and irresponsible-making destruction, whose most certain effect would be to leave everything as it is and to consolidate the most immobile forces.[66]

This point is emphasized by the lack of a gap in Derrida between the political and the "text."[67] Because Derrida does not make the distinction between the constative and the performative, reserving only the former for philosophy, and because he insists *"il n'y a pas de hors-texte,"* then, as Culler argues, "the realities with which politics is concerned, and the forms in which they are manipulated, are inseparable from discursive structures and systems of signification. . . . Dependent upon the hierarchical oppositions of our tradition, they are liable to be affected by inversions and displacements of those hierarchies, though such effects may be slow to work themselves out."[68]

Yet Culler still sees what he calls the "gap" between political work and philosophical or theoretical deconstruction as problematic because "attempts to reverse and thus displace major hierarchical oppositions of western thought open possibilities of change that are incalculable."[69] Culler argues for a retention of the "gap," as the future to which the political application of deconstruction would lead is not obviously progressive: For example, "an apparently specialised or perverse investigation may transform a whole domain by inverting and displacing the oppositions that made its concerns marginal."[70]

Another key question raised when deconstructive approaches are debated in a political context is the strategic need for an inversion of the hierarchy of oppositional terms. For example, the question for feminists is whether to obscure or assert the difference between man and woman, "male" and "female."[71] Do they demonstrate that women can do anything men can, or do they claim that women are superior to men and that women's values should become dominant? Disagreements over these issues within feminism and the feminist movement have been severe. Deconstruction suggests another approach, working on both fronts at once: "Analytical writings that attempt to neutralise the male/female opposition are extremely important, but . . . a movement that asserts the primacy of the oppressed term is strategically indispensable."[72]

This is a particularly useful example of how the strategies of deconstruction impact on the political. The argument is that the promotion of the feminine should not take place alone but should be accompanied by the deconstructive attempt to displace the sexual opposition. In Shoshana Felman's words: "Femininity as real otherness . . . is uncanny in that it is not the opposite of masculinity but that which subverts the very opposition of masculinity and femininity."[73] The deconstructive approach leads to a new concept of "woman" that subverts the ideological distinction between man and woman, much as Derrida's proto- or archiwriting displaces the ordinary distinction between speech and writing. As Julia Kristeva puts it: "We must use 'we are women' as an advertisement or slogan for our demands. On a deeper level, however, a woman is not something one can 'be'; it does not even belong to the order of being. . . . By 'woman' I understand what cannot be represented, what is not said, what remains above and beyond nomenclatures and ideologies."[74]

Some feminists are clearly concerned with the implications of the conclusion that "'woman' may no longer refer to actual human beings defined by historical representations of sexual identity but serves rather as the horizon of a critique identifying 'sexual identity,' 'representation,' and the 'subject' as ideological impositions."[75] This is the other front of the struggle that involves the celebration of the work of women. Derrida's question is how to reduce the gap between the two fronts without sacrificing one to the other. The struggle needs to be continued on both fronts at once.

Another example of the political impact of deconstruction can be seen in relation to discussions of famine relief. Recent work on humanitarian intervention and famines has called into question the role of relief, particularly where conflict is involved.[76] Does relief benefit the victims of famines, or rather, does it serve to perpetuate famines, through its diversion to military purposes, feeding soldiers, and the like? Or more radically, perhaps, does famine relief in fact benefit the donors and others who anyway profit from famine more than those threatened with starvation? Perhaps relief aid actually causes famine, by encouraging and rewarding actions taken by one group, which is attempting for political reasons, because of conflict over resources or control, to starve another. This argument has led to new guidelines for relief efforts and a call to "do no harm." The impact of relief is to be measured and analyzed more carefully.

But to regard famine relief as the cause rather than the solution of famine is merely to invert the oppositions inherent to an approach that seeks, in a logocentric manner, for solutions in terms of cause and effect. What is needed, it has been argued, is to make the move that treats relief as the undecidable—and hence political.[77] This argument, and the discussion of the violence inherent in "law," draws on Derrida's work on the force of law and the undecidable/political, which is the subject of the next section. This work is central to my argument in relation to depoliticization and technologization. Whereas some see Derrida's work as apolitical or "conservative," I believe that it is, on the contrary, conceptualizations such as undecidability that reveal how logocentric approaches depoliticize through their claims to knowledge and through technologization.

FORCE OF LAW AND UNDECIDABILITY

An understanding of Derrida's notion of the "force" inherent in the "violent hierarchy" of binary oppositions is helpful in discussing deconstruction and the political. It can be clarified by looking at his work on the "force of law." Derrida draws attention to two aspects of the "force of law"—the force of enforcement, which goes along with the possibility of "law," and the violent force of law's foundational moment. The first of these inevitably accompanies the law: "The word 'enforceability' reminds us that there is no such thing as law (*droit*) that doesn't imply *in itself, a priori, in the analytic structure of its concept,* the possibility of being 'enforced,' applied by force." [78] The force of enforcement is always legitimate, authorized by what Weber would call, as we saw in Chapter 1, "legal rational authority." But this is not the same thing as saying that the law is just; the enforcement of law is always deemed legitimate even if at the same time it is recognized as unjust. As Derrida puts it, "Law is always an authorized force, a force that justifies itself or is justified in applying itself, even if this justification may be judged from elsewhere to be unjust or unjustifiable."[79] One obeys laws because they are the law: Anyone who obeys them because they are just is not obeying them the way one ought to.[80] Derrida claims that we can find in this the basis for "a critique of juridical ideology" that would show the way the layers of the law "hide and reflect" the interests of the dominant forces in society.

Such a critique would be useful, but we can move beyond it to examine the second aspect of the force of law, which concerns the way in which the law, in its very founding moment, the moment that institutes the law as such, as legal system, implies a performative force. This is not the type of force involved in the enforcement of law, by a preexisting, external social power but a "performative and therefore interpretative violence that in itself is neither just nor unjust and that no previous law . . . could guarantee or contradict or invalidate."[81]

Arguably, what we have here, in what Derrida describes as a "sense of law that would maintain a more internal, more complex relation with what one calls force, power or violence,"[82] is a link between *logos* and force that recalls Foucault's power/knowledge link (discussed in the previous chapter). This connection, for Derrida, takes place through undecidability. The undecidable is not just the oscillation between contradictions, such as between a universal right and the singularity of a particular "unsubsumable" example. It is not merely the tension or oscillation between two decisions. It lies in the process of the decision itself: "The undecidable is . . . the experience of that which . . . is . . . obliged . . . to give itself up to the impossible decision, while taking account of laws and rules."[83] It is found in "the moment of suspense"[84] at which the decision has not yet been taken.

We can explore this further by looking at Derrida's discussion of "justice." The concept of justice, or the "just" act, requires both the notion of freedom (an act without freedom and responsibility could not be said to be just or unjust) and the notion of following a rule or prescription (for example, of the law). This recalls Foucault again, this time his view of the resistance without which there are no relations of power and its connection with freedom. But to return to Derrida, the mere application of a rule or law, if there could be such a thing, would not be "just"; it would be merely legal. This is similar to the distinction I made in Chapter 1 between "politics" seen as a technical (and technically irresponsible) action within an existing framework, and "the political," the act that institutes or reproduces the framework. What is needed for justice is something different:

> To be just, the decision of a judge, for example, must not only follow the law but must also assume it, approve it, confirm its value, by a reinstituting act of interpretation, as if ultimately nothing previously existed of the law. . . . Each case is other, each decision is different and requires an absolutely unique interpretation, which no existing, coded rule can or ought to guarantee absolutely.[85]

Because of the uniqueness of a particular instance, each decision involves the reinvention of the law to fit the case—a new reading that cannot claim to be completely derived from rule or precedent. Such a decision would be "just" in that it would be a nontechnical, responsible act, not following a rule. But once a decision is taken, we cannot say whether it is just or not, precisely because the notion of "just" is caught in the moment of the undecidable. Here the role of a nonlinear notion of time is crucial. There is a black hole that conceals the moment of decision and means that we cannot tell whether it has taken place or not. To quote Derrida here:

> A decision that [was] only the programmable application . . . of a calculable process . . . might be legal; it would not be just. But in the moment of suspense of the undecidable it is not just either, for only a decision is just. . . . And once the ordeal of the undecidable is past . . . the decision has again followed a rule or given itself a rule. . . . It is no longer presently just, fully just. There is apparently no moment in which a decision can be called presently and fully just: either it has not yet been made according to a rule, and nothing allows us to call it just, or it has already followed a rule—whether received, confirmed, conserved or reinvented—which in its turn is not absolutely guaranteed by anything; and, moreover, if it were guaranteed, the decision would be reduced to calculation and we couldn't call it just.[86]

In other words, once the moment of decision has past (assuming, since we cannot know, that there was one), the rule that the decision appears to have followed has already been invented. In this sense, although the "ordeal of the undecidable" must be gone through—the decision must be taken—this decision does not in any sense "overcome" the undecidable: "The undecidable remains caught, lodged, at least as a ghost—but an essential ghost—in every decision, in every event of decision. Its ghostliness deconstructs from within any assurance of presence . . . that would assure us . . . of the very event of a decision."[87] This notion of the undecidable can be compared to Lacan's *point de capiton:* where a moment, a present, never exists and yet retroactively is produced as it always has been.[88] The temporality of the future anterior, the "will have been," is seen here also.

We can further clarify the moment of decision by looking at the revolutionary moment and the founding of the state (the law):[89] I discussed this in Chapter 1 as the moment of the political, the instant of the founding of a law that is not legitimized by the previous state or legal system. It goes out on a limb, so to speak. If the revolutionaries fail, they will be arrested and charged by the state as criminals or terrorists. If, however, they succeed, and a new state is instituted, it will appear retroactively as if their actions had been totally justified. As Derrida puts it,

> All revolutionary situations, all revolutionary discourses, on the left or on the right, . . . justify the recourse to violence by alleging the founding, in progress or to come, of a new law. As this law to come will in return legitimate, retrospectively, the violence that may offend the sense of justice, its future anterior already justifies it.[90]

Derrida, like Žižek, *relates this situation to the ideological,* to the role of the knowledge/ignorance, consciousness/unconsciousness of the participants to what is happening in an elusive present. They are "feigning the presence" while they "do not know very well, by definition, what they are saying." But this ignorance is crucial, according to Derrida: "It is precisely in this ignorance that the eventness of the event consists, what we naively call its presence."[91] The terrifying moments are indecipherable; this is what Montaigne called "the mystical foundation of authority," a moment that "always takes place and never takes place in presence."[92] The subject in this moment of suspense, this founding moment, is in a situation of paradox with respect to the law. The law is yet to come, but to come through the performative act of the subject through which it is instituted but of which there is no "present": "The law is transcendent and theological, and so always to come, always promised, because it is immanent, finite and so already past. Every 'subject' is caught up in this aporetic structure in advance."[93]

CONCLUSION

It is at the point at which we begin to look at undecidability and the political, then, that we see most clearly the connection between Derrida's deconstruction and my exploration of politics and the political in Chapter 1. As I noted at the start, however, the logic of undecidability, which is the logic of the political, was present in Derrida's work from the beginning, in his analysis of logocentrism and *différance.* I have also demonstrated the links between this work and power/knowledge and resistance in Foucault and the "ideological" in Žižek. I return to these points in Chapter 7 when I discuss in more detail the notions of repoliticization and the political. By opening to inspection the notion of the undecidable—the foundational moment of hierarchy (and "politics")—deconstruction is entering the terrain of the political. It is also the terrain of ideology. The force of law and the legitimacy of authority rely on its foundational moment remaining if not hidden, at least unacknowledged. As Chapter 6 shows, this is similar to Žižek's notion of the ideological as implicated in the very existence of (what we call) social reality.

NOTES

1. Jacques Derrida, "Force of Law: The 'Mystical Foundation of Authority,'" in *Deconstruction and the Possibility of Justice,* ed. David Gray Carlson, Drucilla Cornell, and Michel Rosenfeld, trans. Mary Quaintance (New York: Routledge, 1992), 21.

2. Jacques Derrida, "Signature Event Context," in *Limited Inc,* ed. Jacques Derrida, trans. Samuel Weber and Jeffrey Mehlman (Evanston, IL: Northwestern University Press, 1988), 1–23.

3. Jacques Derrida, *Writing and Difference,* trans. Alan Bass (London: Routledge, 1978).

4. Barbara Johnson, "Translator's Introduction," in Jacques Derrida, *Dissemination* (London: Athlone Press, 1981), vii–ix.

5. Jacques Derrida, *Of Grammatology,* trans. Gayatri Chakravorty Spivak (Baltimore, MD: Johns Hopkins University Press, 1976), 3.

6. Jonathan Culler, *On Deconstruction: Theory and Criticism After Structuralism* (London: Routledge, 1983), 92.

7. Ibid., 93.

8. Rousseau quoted in Derrida, *Of Grammatology,* 296.

9. Derrida, *Of Grammatology,* 296.

10. Ibid., 295, 298.

11. For discussions of quantum mechanics and relativity, see, for example, P. C. W. Davies and J. R. Brown, *The Ghost in the Atom: A Discussion of the Mysteries of Quantum Mechanics* (Cambridge: Cambridge University Press, 1986); Alastair I. M. Rae, *Quantum Physics: Illusion or Reality?* (Cambridge: Cambridge University Press, 1986); Albert Einstein, *Relativity: The Special and the General Theory,* trans. Robert W. Lawson (London: Methuen, 1920).

12. Culler, *On Deconstruction,* 95.

13. Jacques Derrida, *Margins of Philosophy,* trans. Alan Bass (Chicago: University of Chicago Press, 1982), 16. The implications of this move for the notion of the subject are fundamental: "The category of the subject cannot be, and never has been, thought without the reference to presence. . . . The privilege granted to consciousness signifies the privilege granted to the present" (ibid.).

14. Culler, *On Deconstruction,* 95.

15. Ibid., 96.

16. Johnson, "Introduction," ix.

17. See also the extensive footnote in *Positions* where Derrida discusses his relation to Lacan. Jacques Derrida, *Positions,* trans. Alan Bass (London: Athlone Press, 1987), 107–113.

18. Culler, *On Deconstruction,* 161.

19. Ibid., 162.

20. Ibid.

21. Derrida, *Margins*, 20–21.

22. Derrida, *Writing and Difference,* 203.

23. Ibid., 211–212.

24. Derrida, *Positions,* 42–43.

25. Ibid., 43.

26. Ibid., 101.

27. Culler, *On Deconstruction,* 103.

28. Henry Staten, *Wittgenstein and Derrida* (Oxford: Blackwell, 1984).

29. Derrida, *Of Grammatology,* 157.

30. Culler, *On Deconstruction,* 105.

31. Derrida, *Of Grammatology,* 8.

32. Culler, *On Deconstruction,* 109.

33. Staten, *Wittgenstein and Derrida.*

34. Ibid., 16.

35. Culler, *On Deconstruction,* 120.

36. Ibid., 123.

37. Ibid., 135.

38. Rodolphe Gasché, *The Tain of the Mirror: Derrida and the Philosophy of Reflection* (Cambridge: Harvard University Press, 1986), 138–139. According to Gasché, deconstruction attempts "to 'account' for these 'contradictions' by 'grounding' them in 'infrastructures' discovered by analyzing the specific organization of these 'contradictions'" (ibid., 142). Clarifying the meanings of "structure" and "infrastructure" should help us understand the epistemological achievement of deconstruction. Derrida's notion of *différance* is one example of "infrastructures." This notion is not the same as the traditional concept of structure, which is always centered and which originated in a concept of spatiality. To get around this we have the concept of the structurality of structure, which attempts, among other things, a decentering.

39. Derrida, *Positions,* 41.

40. Johnson, "Introduction," xiii.

41. Culler, *On Deconstruction,* 88.

42. Derrida, *Of Grammatology,* 158–159.

43. Derrida, *Writing and Difference,* 280–281.

44. Johnson, "Introduction," xvi.

45. Ibid., xiv.

46. Ibid., xv.

47. Gasché, *Tain of the Mirror,* 168.

48. Derrida, *Writing and Difference,* 281.

49. Gasché, *Tain of the Mirror,* 174.

50. Culler, *On Deconstruction,* 150.

51. Ibid., 150–151.

52. Ibid., 213–214.

53. Derrida, "Signature Event Context."

54. "Limited Inc a b c . . . ," in Derrida, *Limited Inc.,* 29–110.

55. Derrida, "Signature Event Context," 4.

56. Ibid., 10.

57. Ibid., 12.

58. Ibid., 13–14.

59. Ibid., 14.

60. Ibid., 15.

61. Ibid.

62. Ibid., 17.

63. Ibid., 18.

64. Ibid., 20 (my emphasis).

65. Ibid., 21.

66. Jacques Derrida, "The Conflict of Faculties," in *Languages of Knowledge and of Inquiry*, ed. Michael Riffaterre (New York: Columbia University Press, 1982), quoted in Culler, *On Deconstruction*, 156.

67. Or what, as we have just seen, he calls the "expansion of *a general writing*"; Derrida, "Signature Event Context," 20 (my emphasis).

68. Culler, *On Deconstruction*, 157.

69. Ibid., 158.

70. Ibid., 159.

71. See Chapter 2 for further elaboration of these points.

72. Culler, *On Deconstruction*, 173.

73. Shoshana Felman, "Rereading Femininity," *Yale French Studies*, 62 (1981): 42, quoted in Culler, *On Deconstruction*, 174.

74. Julia Kristeva, "La Femme, ce n'est jamais ça," *Tel quel* 59 (1974): 20–21; partial translation as Julia Kristeva, "Woman Cannot Be Defined," in *New French Feminisms*, ed. Elaine Marks and Isabelle de Courtivron (Amherst: University of Massachusetts Press, 1980), 137–138; quoted in Culler, *On Deconstruction*, 174–175. Again, see the discussion of Luce Irigaray in Chapter 2.

75. Culler, *On Deconstruction*, 175.

76. Jenny Edkins, "Legality with a Vengeance: Famines and Humanitarian Intervention in 'Complex Emergencies,'" *Millennium*, 25, 3 (1996): 547–575.

77. Ibid., 570.

78. Derrida, "Force of Law," 5–6.

79. Ibid.

80. This is similar to the point Žižek makes. Slavoj Žižek, *The Sublime Object of Ideology* (London: Verso, 1989), 37.

81. Derrida, "Force of Law," 13.

82. Ibid.

83. Ibid., 24.

84. Ibid., 13.

85. Ibid., 23.

86. Ibid., 24.

87. Ibid., 24–25.

88. Derrida hesitates in his use of terms such as "symbolic" for fear of the Lacanian links these produce. Ibid., 37.

89. This reading of Walter Benjamin forms the second part of the "Force of Law." As we saw at the beginning of the chapter, deconstruction has two modes. The "Force of Law" essay exemplifies these, using an examination of philosophical concepts in its first section and a reading of a text in its second.

90. Derrida, "Force of Law," 35. In this context the Velvet Revolution in Czechoslovakia and nonviolent revolutions in other former Communist states are interesting. Žižek can help us throw some light on this when he discusses how in Communist Yugoslavia legitimation of the state was founded on a double entendre, an ideology that relied on nonbelief that was concealed.

91. Derrida, "Force of Law," 35.

92. Ibid., 36.

93. Ibid.

5

The Lacanian Subject

The Lacanian approach to the subject, ideology, and "social reality" of Slovenian philosopher Slavoj Žižek locates ideology in the problematic of consciousness or subjectivity as such and enables us to analyze how the ideological and depoliticization are linked. Marxism, at least in its class-centered form, places ideology as part of the concealment of the alienation of the subject from his or her productive activity. The political antagonism inherent in the process of capitalism is "obscured" by bourgeois ideology.[1] For Foucault, discursive practices are bound up with the production and reproduction of relations of power in society. "Régimes of truth" are political: They reflect and constitute relations of domination, and practices of discipline produce subjects as objects of knowledge.[2] But in his work on the ethics of existence, Foucault believes it is still possible for the subject to create him- or herself as a harmonious ethical subject.[3]

For Žižek, a Lacanian approach leads to a picture of ideology at the level of the social as concealing the inherently antagonistic nature of *all* attempts at society (which, as I discussed in Chapter 1, would be to depoliticize by concealing the political), and at the level of the subject as enabling the subject to constitute him- or herself, despite the constitutive lack that lies at the root of (self-)consciousness. The role of the ideological is closely linked with the (impossible) aim of producing (what we call) a meaningful "social reality" (the domain of "politics") and thus concealing the traumatic "real." In Chapter 2 I took up Hall's argument that the subject had been decentered, with the Cartesian subject becoming fragmented and split, and I traced this through the work of Freud, Saussure, and Marx.[4] In Žižek's work on ideology, not only is the subject fragmented and split, but the symbolic order at the basis of social reality is itself "impossible," incomplete and constituted by an inherent "lack." This argument draws on Laclau and Mouffe's work on antagonism and the impossibility of society, which I discuss further in Chapter 7.[5] Ideology, in the form of social fantasy, serves to respond to and conceal this lack or antagonism. In Chapter 6 I analyze how this approach changes our understanding of the political. In the present chapter I introduce the work of Lacan, upon which Žižek draws extensively. In particular, I look at Lacan's mirror stage and the graph of desire.[6]

Lacan's writing spans a period from 1930 to 1981, although his work was interrupted by the war and his paper on the mirror stage, first presented in 1936, did not gain recognition until it was published much later, in 1949.[7] He trained as a clinical psychiatrist, and his work was explicitly Freudian. He came into conflict with the Société Psychoanalytique de Paris over his method of analysis using "short sessions"; in 1953 he broke with the official Freudian establishment. At the same time, he began a series of annual seminars that continued for the next twenty-seven years. In 1964 he founded the École Freudienne de Paris—only to dissolve it in 1980 amid protest. He was a controversial figure, and his writing is reputed to be deliberately unintelligible: "I like . . . to leave the reader no other way out than the way in, which I prefer to be difficult."[8] His use of "mathemes" and elaborate diagrams is part of this style.

There have been various distinct uses of Lacan.[9] In France the clinical application of his work has been prominent, and this aspect has remained central despite the broader spread of Lacan's work and attempts to articulate it with other theoretical approaches—the work of Althusser within Marxism, for example. In the Anglo-Saxon world, the clinical aspect of his writing has been overshadowed by its use in literature, cinema studies, and feminism. This work has seen Lacan in general terms as part of poststructuralism and emphasized his affinities with Derridean deconstruction. As well as the contrasts between different countries, there are also discrepancies between different "schools" of Lacanian thought. Those based on his early work tend to highlight his more "structuralist" approach to the imaginary and the symbolic, whereas theorists who play up his later work give a central role to the notion of the "Real" as that which resists symbolization.

The Slovenian school of which Žižek is a key figure is original in its use of Lacan in a philosophical and political context and in particular in its work on the theorization of ideology. The Slovenian school uses Lacan in the analysis of classic philosophical texts and to give a new reading of G. W. F. Hegel. A large number of works have already appeared in Slovenian, with some translations into French. Since 1989 Žižek has published books in various languages, including English.[10] His work is increasingly widely recognized in the Anglo-Saxon world, though little in the way of a secondary literature has yet appeared.[11] Žižek was very much involved in the democratization movements in Slovenia in the late 1980s and early 1990s, standing as a pro-reform candidate for the presidency of Slovenia in 1990. According to Peter Dews, it is "the political context which explains the intellectual investment of Žižek and his colleagues in a Lacanian reading of Hegel."[12] They were driven by the need to find a critical approach to the system in Yugoslavia, a system that was manipulative and deceptive in the name of an ideology that denounced manipulation and deception.

Žižek claims that it is because of the way Hegel deals with the notion of antagonism that Hegelianism is central to his approach. For Marx, class antagonism is fundamental and ontologically prior; historical development brings the possibility of solving this fundamental antagonism (and hence all others). A similar argument—though one that sees a different fundamental antagonism in each case—is found in feminism, ecology, and democracy. Post-Marxists such as Laclau and Chantal Mouffe break with this logic and assert the "irreducible plurality of particular struggles."[13] Their claim, as I examine in Chapter 7, is that the articulation of particular struggles depends on contingency.

Lacanian psychoanalysis goes further than post-Marxism, according to Žižek. The irreducible plurality recognized by post-Marxism arises, for Lacan, because of many responses to the same impossible-real kernel. There is a "radical negativity [that] cannot be reduced to an expression of alienated social conditions, [since] it defines *la condition humaine* as such: there is no solution, no escape from it."[14] Culture can be seen as an attempt to limit, to cultivate this radical antagonism. But "the aspiration to abolish it is precisely the source of totalitarian temptation."[15] For Žižek, the successful solution of a particular problem entails an acknowledgment of the global radical deadlock or impossibility, the acknowledgment of a fundamental antagonism.

LACAN'S MIRROR STAGE

The Freudian decentering of the Cartesian subject was discussed in Chapter 2, especially the way in which consciousness became an aspect of the unconscious. We have seen Freud's two topographies, the first identifying the conscious, preconscious, and unconscious and the second the id, ego, and superego. In both topographies there is a dynamic relationship and conflict between the "agencies."

The role of the ego was not clear in the first topography. Freud conceived it in a new way with the introduction of the concept of narcissism: The unified ego was not present from birth but had to be developed. But how this happens was not clear in Freud. Lacan's mirror stage gives an account that fills the gap.[16] As described in Chapter 2, Freud sees the subject as decentered and marked by a "lack." Lacan follows Freud in this.[17] As will become clear, Lacan moves from the "individualist" orientation of Freud to a more social view, with the concept of the big Other (the symbolic order). He does this by incorporating Saussurean insights concerning language into his work alongside Freudian concepts of the unconscious.

The mirror stage introduces ideas of (self-)consciousness as founded on (mis)recognition and on the illusion that is inherent in "*la condition humaine* as such" and from which there is no escape. The mirror stage sees the formation of the ego as an *imaginary* relation. The graph of desire explores how Lacanian subjectivity implicates the social order. This gives an account of the formation of the subject as distinct from the ego, and this takes place at the level of the symbolic.

Lacan's account of the formation of the "I" through what he calls the mirror stage is based on the observation that a child between the ages of six and eighteen months can recognize his or her image in a mirror. Having recognized the image, the child goes on to "play" with it, watching how the movements he or she makes are reflected in the image and so on.[18] Lacan interprets this mirror stage as a process of identification.[19] The mirror stage is "the symbolic matrix in which the 'I' is precipitated in a primordial form, before it is objectified in the dialectic of identification with the other, and before language restores to it, in the universal, its function as subject."[20]

This account is significant in that the formation of the ego exhibits a number of characteristics. First, it is fictional; it institutes for the ego a discordance with its own reality. The infant sees a whole, complete, "total" body in contrast to its own disconnected movements and lack of control. The mirror stage functions to "establish a relation between the organism and its reality."[21] But at the point when this relation is established, the "fragmented body-image" of the infant contrasts starkly with the totality of the reflection presented in the mirror. This discontinuity, which arises from the prematurity of human birth, has, according to Lacan, long-term effects on the subject's mental development, which produce a succession of fantasies and experiences of alienation:

> The *mirror stage* is a drama whose internal thrust is precipitated from insufficiency to anticipation—and which manufactures for the subject, caught up in the lure of spatial identification, the succession of fantasies that extends from a fragmented body-image to a form of its totality . . . —and, lastly to the assumption of the armour of an alienating identity, which will mark the rigid structure of the subject's entire mental development.[22]

This "totality" is the second crucial characteristic.[23]

Lacan seems to regard the mirror stage of development as "presocial," although it cannot take place without the infant's being "held tightly by some support, human or artificial."[24] It also seems likely, according to

John Muller and William Richardson, that the "mirror" is not meant to be taken literally: Identification can take place through the infant's perceiving his or her "reflection" in a human caregiver. The disjuncture of this preformed self with the social occurs later:

> [The] moment in which the mirror stage comes to an end inaugurates . . . the dialectic that will . . . link the "I" to socially elaborated situations. It is this moment that decisively tips the whole of human knowledge into mediatisation through the desire of the other, constitutes its objects in an abstract equivalence by the co-operation of others, and turns the "I" into that apparatus for which every instinctual thrust constitutes a danger, even though it should correspond to a natural maturation.[25]

The mirror image is a totality, a gestalt, which can be mastered. This imaginary mastery anticipates the biological mastery of the infant's body he or she has not yet achieved. For Lacan, the formation of the ego commences at this point. It is based on an imaginary relationship of the individual to his or her body. The images of the fragmented body from earlier months are linked to aggressivity. The mirror image inaugurates a relation between the infant and the world around him or her, as seen in the image. This is discordant "because it is based on an imaginary and alienating experience."[26] Aggressivity is a "correlative tension of the narcissistic structure in the coming-into-being of the subject."[27] it is released in any relation with the other, "even in a relation involving the most Samaritan of aid."[28]

We see from this account of the mirror stage that the role of illusion in the formation of the ego is crucial. A continuing search for an imaginary completeness is one of its outcomes. For Lacan, the aim of psychoanalytic treatment was not to enable the individual to adjust better to his or her surroundings, to strengthen the ego, or anything similar.[29] As a result of the mirror stage, the ego's mastery of its environment will *always* be illusory: "The human subject will continue throughout life to look for an imaginary 'wholeness' and 'unity.' . . . These quests . . . are futile."[30]

It is not just in the formation of consciousness or the ego in childhood that Lacan connects subjectivity with questions of illusion and (mis)recognition. His writings on how consciousness and subjectivity work in a more general way provide an approach that contrasts with theories of ideology and the subject I have considered so far. The graphs of desire demonstrate this point, as it is here that the connection with language (or what Lacan calls the symbolic order) comes in. Lacan's work on the unconscious is based on Freud but draws on processes discussed in Saussure's linguistics. Below I introduce a number of concepts crucial for rethinking the political and ideology: the notion of interpellation and the *point de capiton,* the relations of temporality, and the relation to the big Other (the symbolic order).

According to Lacan, Freud decentered the fully conscious self much as Copernicus and Darwin decentered humans within the world. "Since Freud the unconscious has been a chain of signifiers that somewhere (on another stage, in another scene, he wrote) is repeated, and insists on interfering in the breaks offered it by the effective discourse and the cogitation that it informs."[31] The term "signifier," Lacan points out, was not available to Freud but comes from modern linguistics, structuralism, and formalism. There are parallels between Freudian theory and structural linguistics: "The mechanisms described by Freud as those of the primary process, in which the unconscious assumes its rule, correspond exactly to the functions that this school believes determine the most radical aspects of the effects of language, namely metaphor and metonymy—in other words, the signifier's effects of substitution and combination on the respectively synchronic and diachronic dimensions in which they appear in discourse."[32] The reference here is to the mechanisms of displacement and condensation, which Lacan links with those of metaphor and metonymy. So we arrive at Lacan's crucial claim, which is that "the unconscious is structured like a language."[33]

The question Lacan asks then becomes: "Once the structure of language has been recognised in the unconscious, what sort of subject can we conceive for it?"[34] In other words, what are the implications of this psychoanalytical approach—which sees the unconscious structured as a language—for the theory of the subject and subjectivity? What notion of the subject does this lead us to? Lacan proceeds to explore the relation of signifier to signified and the constitution of the subject through the use of a series of graphs that illustrate the topography of the relationship in increasing, eventually multilayered complexity.

As we saw in the discussion of general linguistics in Chapter 2, Saussure pictured the relation between signifier and signified as two undulating surfaces sliding over each other (Figure 5.1), fixed temporarily and contingently in the sign, a particular (arbitrary) relation between signifier and signified. Lacan's view is shown in the first level of the graph of desire (Figure 5.2); this gives an initial picture of his view of the subject and interpellation.[35] In Saussure's diagram the subdivision (shown by the dotted lines) of the plane of jumbled ideas (A) and the equally vague plane of sounds (B) produces order: "Thought . . . has to become ordered in the process of its divisions."[36] The process of division produces the units and their articulation.

In Lacan's graph, the plane of the signifier is represented by the vector SS'. The chain of signifiers has its motion arrested, for the time being, by the retroactive motion of another vector, $\Delta \mathcal{S}$, which quilts the signifier's chain. This retroactively produces the subject, which is the Lacanian barred split subject ($\mathcal{S}$). This is the process of interpellation of individuals

Figure 5.1   Saussure's Diagram

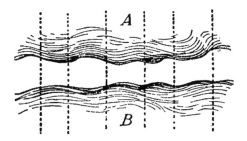

Source: From *Cours de Linguistique Generale,* Ferdinand de Saussure, published by Charles Bally and Albert Sechehaye, with the collaboration of Albert Riedlinger, 1949. Reprinted by permission of Éditions Payot et Rivages, Paris.

Figure 5.2   Lacan's Graph I

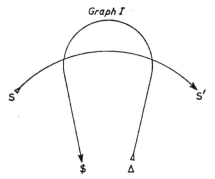

Source: From *Écrits: A Selection* by Jacques Lacan, translated by Alan Sheridan. Copyright © 1966 by Editions Du Seuil. English translation copyright © 1977 by Tavistock Publications. Reprinted in the U.S. and Canada by permission of W. W. Norton & Company, Inc. Reprinted in the rest of the world by permission of Routledge.

into subjects. As Žižek puts it, "The *point de capiton* [quilting point] is the point through which the subject is 'sewn' into the signifier, and at the same time the point which interpellates individual into subject by addressing it with the call of a certain master-signifier ('Communism,' 'God,' 'Freedom,' 'America')—in a word it is the point of subjectivation of the signifier's chain."[37] Crucially, this retroactive process of signification produces the illusion of an element present in the signifier as its very essence, from the beginning, as we saw in the mirror stage: "The . . . 'quilting' . . . is successful only in so far as it effaces its own traces."[38] What we have is not the unfolding of a preexisting meaning, and essence, but the retroactive production of meaning, a "radically contingent process."[39]

So with this emphasis on retroactive production of meaning, the notion of interpellation follows the temporal structure introduced into subjectivity in the mirror stage: "The mirror . . . supplies . . . an image of the future and the subject identifies with what it will become."[40] Interpellation can be formulated in terms where language, as the *always already* perhaps, is the catalyst:

> The function of language is not to inform but to evoke. . . . What I seek in speech is the response of the other. What constitutes me as subject is my question. In order to be recognised by the other, I utter what *was* only in view of what *will be*. In order to find him, I call him by a name he must assume or refuse in order to reply to me. . . . I identify myself in language, but only by losing myself in it like an object. What is realised in my history is not the past definite of what *was*, since it is no more, or even the present perfect of what *has been* in what I am, but the future anterior of what I *shall have been* for what I am in the process of becoming.[41]

As well as the role of temporality in the production of the subject, Lacan also draws our attention to how the process implicates power relations and the political. The basis of interpellation is authoritarian: "If I call the person to whom I am speaking by whatever name I choose to give him, I intimate to him the subjective function that he will take on again in order to reply to me, even if it is to repudiate this function."[42]

The first graph succinctly expresses the retroactive form of subjectivity. It draws on an analogy with embroidery and the process of quilting, where a backward stitch anchors together layers of fabric. In the process of signification, "the signifier stops the otherwise endless movement (*glissement*) of the signification."[43] In other words, the sliding of the signification is briefly and temporarily arrested by the retroactive action of the signifier. The anchoring point is called the "point de capiton," or quilting point. An illustration of the retroactive way this works is given by the example of the sentence. As Lacan puts it, "The diachronic function of this anchoring point is to be found in the sentence, even if the sentence completes its signification only with its last term, each term being anticipated in the construction of the others, and inversely, sealing their meaning by its retroactive effect."[44] The meaning of the sentence, and of each term within it, only *becomes* what it *is* when the sentence is complete.

There are two points, then, to emphasize from this discussion of the first graph, and I pick these up in the sections below. The first is the way the subject is constituted by interpellation and the way this operates retroactively. The second, implicit rather than explicit in the discussion so far, is an argument about naming. As discussed below, Žižek, following the notions introduced here, argues that it is the retroactive effect of naming that supports the identity of an object. Naming is the discursive construction of the object itself, as interpellation constitutes the subject. For

Figure 5.3   Lacan's Graph II

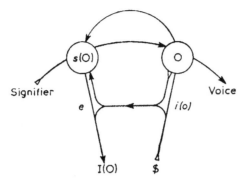

Laclau, this means that "the essentially performative character of naming is the precondition for all hegemony and politics."[45]

In the second graph (Figure 5.3), Lacan introduces several new elements, of which the most important to our discussion is the locus of the Other. The big Other (the symbolic order or "synchronous symbolic code") is introduced at the first cross point of the original two vectors, and the signified s(O) at the second. The rest of the graph expresses in more detail the same processes we saw in the first graph. As we have seen, "Meaning . . . is produced . . . backwards from the point at which the relation between the floating signifiers is fixed through reference to the synchronous symbolic code."[46] The axis *ei(o)* represents the mirror stage, which can be described as the "imaginary" level that supports the illusion of the self as autonomous agent. The subject is again shown as constituted retroactively.

This process involves (and produces) a (mis)recognition: "a failure to recognise that is essential to knowing myself (*un méconnaître essential au me connaître*) is introduced . . . the transcendental ego itself is relativised, implicated . . . in the *méconnaissance* in which the ego's identifications take root."[47] The dimension of (mis)recognition (*méconnaissance*) is inherent in the constitution of the subject. I return to this in my discussion of ideology in the next chapter.

The third graph (Figure 5.4) introduces a further aspect—the notion of a certain gap, an unanswered question, which according to Žižek emerges in the interplay of imaginary and symbolic identification. It is at this third level that Lacan's work leads to an approach that departs most markedly from other approaches to the subject and ideology. The distinction between imaginary identification and symbolic identification is that between the

Figure 5.4   Lacan's Graph III

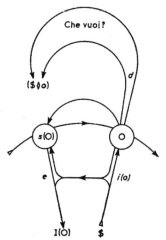

ideal ego *i(o),* which is what we would like to be, and the ego-ideal I(O), which is the agency through which we judge ourselves. Imaginary identification is identification with the image in which we appear likable to ourselves, and symbolic identification is identification with the very place from which we are observed, from where we look at ourselves so that we appear likable. As Žižek describes it:

> This interplay of imaginary and symbolic identification under the domination of symbolic identification constitutes the mechanism by means of which the subject is integrated into a given socio-symbolic field—the way he/she assumes certain "mandates." . . . The only problem is that this "square of the circle" of interpellation, this circular movement between symbolic and imaginary identification, never comes out without a certain leftover.[48]

The gap that remains is symbolized in the third graph with the question *Che vuoi?* (What do you want?), which Žižek interprets as meaning: "You're telling me that, but what do you want with it, what are you aiming at?"[49]

As a "being-of-language," a human being is always attached to some signifier that represents him or her for the other. It is through this that he or she is given a mandate, "a place in the intersubjective network of symbolic relations." But "this mandate is ultimately always arbitrary: since its real nature is performative, it cannot be accounted for by reference to 'real' properties and capabilities of the subject."[50] The subject then cannot make the link between his or her imaginary or real self and the mandate that places him or her within the symbolic order. The subject is always faced with the unanswerable question, from the Other (the symbolic order), of why he or she has that mandate: The subject does not know why.[51]

The answer to the enigma of the Other's desire (what the Other wants of the subject who has taken on a particular mandate) is given in the graph as fantasy (represented by the Lacanian matheme $\$ \lozenge o$):

> Fantasy functions as a construction, as an imaginary scenario filling out the void, the opening of the desire in the Other: by giving us a definite answer to the question "What does the Other want?" it enables us to evade the unbearable deadlock in which the Other wants something from us but we are at the same time incapable of translating this desire of the Other into a positive interpellation, into a mandate with which to identify.[52]

The final form of the graph of desire (Figure 5.5) includes a new vector: the vector of enjoyment (*jouissance*) intersecting the vector of desire. This is a difficult aspect of Lacan's work to explain; I give here some indication of what is meant, and these questions arise again in the next chapter. The graph now has two levels, the lower being the level of meaning and the upper the level of enjoyment. The first level is, as we have seen, concerned with how the intersection of the signifying chain produces the (retroactive) effect of meaning as a function of the symbolic order. The

Figure 5.5   Lacan's Completed Graph

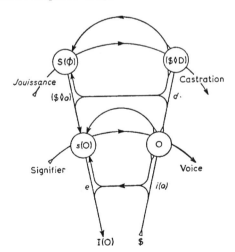

second level represents "what happens when this very field of the signifier's order, of the big Other, is perforated, penetrated by a pre-symbolic (real) stream of enjoyment—what happens when the presymbolic 'substance,' the body as materialised, incarnated enjoyment, becomes enmeshed in the signifier's network."[53] It is the second level that is the key to Lacan's contribution to theories of ideology and the subject. This level is where the real interacts with the symbolic.[54]

The order of the signifier and that of enjoyment (the real) are incompatible. Enjoyment is what cannot be symbolized. The result of their interaction is the dismemberment of the body on the one hand and the exposure of the inconsistency or lack in the symbolic on the other. This leads to "the most radical dimension of Lacanian theory [which] lies . . . in realising that the big Other, the symbolic order itself, is also *barré,* crossed out, by a fundamental impossibility, structured around an impossible-traumatic kernel, around a central lack."[55] It is not only the subject that is "barred," split, fragmented but also the big Other itself (the symbolic order). It is at this point that the role of social fantasy arises: "Fantasy conceals the fact that the Other, the symbolic order, is structured around some traumatic impossibility, around something which cannot be symbolised—i.e. the real of *jouissance:* through fantasy, *jouissance* is domesticated, 'gentrified.'"[56] The link between social fantasy and ideology is explored more fully in the next chapter.

To summarize, this section has explored the Lacanian subject in a fairly abstract way, introducing notions of the *point de capiton,* interpellation, the symbolic order, fantasy, (mis)recognition, and lack. The next section of the chapter begins an elaboration of how Žižek uses these concepts in his work on ideology.

IDEOLOGY AND THE MASTER SIGNIFIER

The *point de capiton* and operation of "quilting" shown in the first level of the graph of desire are pivotal to the elaboration of a Lacanian theory of ideology. Ideological space, according to Žižek, is made up of floating signifiers—a series of unbound, ideological components "whose very identity is 'open,' overdetermined by their articulation into a chain with other elements."[57] Their meaning depends on their connection with other elements—on how the components are articulated.[58] This articulation takes place, according to Laclau and Mouffe, through a "nodal point" that Žižek equates with the Lacanian *point de capiton.* The endless sliding of signifiers is temporarily arrested when, through a process of struggle, elements are successfully articulated in a particular way. "The quilting performs the totalisation by means of which this free floating of ideological elements is halted, fixed—that is to say, by means of which they become parts of the structured network of meaning" or discourse.[59] The very identity of the elements is retroactively determined by their articulation in a particular discursive setting.

Žižek relates this discussion to the whole problem of "naming": How do names refer to the objects they denote? He discusses the dispute between descriptivism (names refer to objects because they bear a certain meaning related to a cluster of descriptive features) and antidescriptivism (names are connected to objects through a "primal baptism" and remain the same even though the descriptive features of the object change entirely). He argues that both positions miss the crucial point—"the radical contingency of naming."[60] Descriptivism misses the symbolic order, and antidescriptivism, in its standard form, misses the fact that what guarantees the identity of an object in all changes of descriptive features is the retroactive effect of naming itself: "Naming itself retroactively constitutes its reference."[61]

Another important outcome of this (and why it is different), however, is the way the act of naming leads to the production of a surplus. The *point de capiton* or nodal point is the word that "as a word, on the level of the signifier itself, unites a field, constitutes its identity: it is, so to speak, the word to which 'things' themselves refer to recognise themselves in their unity."[62] This "inversion" produces a surplus, the object-cause of desire, that unattainable something. An example might make clear the logic of this inversion that produces a surplus. At first the word "famine" appears as a signifier connoting a cluster of supposedly effective properties—"general and widespread shortages of food, leading to widespread death by starvation"—but this is not yet finished. What happens then is that the relation is inverted. We say that it is like this *because* it is a famine. This inversion, "it is like this because it is a famine," then leads to "well, it is not really quite like this yet"—we have not yet seen widespread deaths, for example. In other words, reality does not measure up to the image. What we have is that "unattainable something" that is in famine more than famine. The process of naming has produced places within the symbolic order that things occupy. But the real does not neatly fit the symbolic space; slotting things into the symbolic order is necessary but always, according to Lacan, produces this effect of a nonsymbolizable surplus.

To repeat this another way, we could say that the radical contingency of naming implies a gap between the real and modes of its symbolization: A certain historical event can be symbolized in a number of ways—the real itself does not provide the symbolization. The surplus, or impossible-real kernel, that which is in an object more than the object, is *produced by the signifying operation*. It is this that stays the same under all counterfactual circumstances—however much the properties linked with the object may change—because it is not real anyway.

All naming is the result of a struggle for ideological hegemony: "The essentialist illusion consists in the belief that it is possible to determine a definite cluster of features, of positive properties, however minimal, which defines the permanent essence" of something; by contrast, according to Žižek, the only way to define something is that it is always designated by the same signifier: "It is the signifier which constitutes the kernel of the object's 'identity.'"[63]

The constitution of identity in this way is a performative, ideological operation. For Žižek, discourse is always to be seen as authoritarian or "political": To form a consistent field of meaning, previously free-floating signifiers are quilted by the master signifier, seen as a paradoxical element that stands for "lack," in "a non-founded founding act of violence."[64] In this, he distinguishes a Lacanian position from that of Jürgen Habermas. In Lacan the master signifier distorts the symbolic field in the very process of establishing it (temporarily) as a discursive field. Without this distortion, the field of meaning would disintegrate: The role of the paradoxical element is constitutive. As Žižek puts it, the master is an impostor—anyone who finds him- or herself at the place of the constitutive lack in the structure will do—but the place it occupies cannot be abolished. It can only be rendered visible as empty. For Habermas, in contrast, disturbances or distortions of rational argument are contingent; discourse itself is inherently nonauthoritarian, and prejudices can be gradually removed to reach an ideal situation of rational exchange of views. For Lacan, if the structural role of the master signifier is suspended, this leads to a state of undecidability.[65]

What appears to be a hindrance, blocking the constitution of the social whole or disrupting rational discourse, is in fact the condition of possibility of any sort of social order or discourse at all. Ideology conceals the constitutive antagonism or lack. This is where ideology critique comes in: "The criticism of ideology must . . . look at the element which holds together the ideological edifice [and] recognise in it the embodiment of a lack, of a chasm of non-sense gaping in the midst of ideological meaning."[66] In ideological discourse the gap between what we wanted to achieve and what happened—the "surplus" of result over intention—is accounted for by what Žižek calls a "meta subject."[67] Examples would be divine providence; the "cunning of reason" as in Hegel; the invisible hand of the market; the objective logic of history; the Jewish conspiracy; patriarchy. This hidden agency, which is (pre)supposed to account for the "surplus," is what Lacan calls the master signifier. It is radically ambivalent, both reassuring and threatening.

The constitution of the subject through processes of interpellation has implications for notions of the subject and subjectivity. Žižek views interpellation as concealing a constitutive "lack": The Lacanian subject is the subject of a lack before it is interpellated into subject positions or subjectivized. The Lacanian notion of the divided subject is, for Žižek, not at all the same as what he calls the "poststructuralist" notion of a series of subject-positions, which supposedly reduces the subject to "subjectiva-tion." The "poststructuralist" subject is "conceived as an effect of a fun-damentally non-subjective process: the subject is always caught in, tra-versed by the pre-subjective process."[68] For Lacan, in contrast, the subject is "an empty place which was filled out with [the different modes of sub-jectivation]; this original void, this lack of symbolic structure, *is* the sub-ject."[69] Thus the subject is opposed to the effect of subjectivation: Subjec-tivation *masks* the lack that is the subject. As Žižek writes:

> The subject is constituted through his own division, splitting, as to the object in him; this object, this traumatic kernel, is the dimension . . . of a "death drive," of a traumatic imbalance, a rooting out. Man as such is "nature sick unto death," derailed, run off the rails through a fascination with a lethal Thing. The process of interpellation-subjectivation is pre-cisely an attempt to elude, to avoid this traumatic kernel through identi-fication: in assuming a symbolic mandate, in recognising himself in the interpellation, the subject evades the dimension of the Thing.[70]

Žižek is claiming that the Lacanian subject, which is divided against itself because of its traumatic kernel, finds in the process of interpellation, of assumption into the symbolic order, a form of oblivion, a "solution" or forgetting of the real, in acceptance of the symbolic, the Other. So the process that for Foucault "produces" the subject as subjectified, the object of domination by the social order, for Lacan conceals the constitutive lack in the subject, the impossible-real kernel.

Žižek contrasts the Lacanian subject with the subject of Foucault's last writings, too. Whereas for Lacan the subject is fundamentally split, barred, for Foucault the subject in *Care of the Self* can shape him- or herself. The personality is a work of art, and the ethics of self-mastery can be used to bring about the harmonization of antagonistic forces. Both Lacan and Fou-cault, Žižek argues, stress the "reverse" that lies behind the "official" ver-sion of the Enlightenment, the reverse of reason and progress and the fissure in Enlightenment universality. For Lacan, the symbolic universe is organized around a void and the subject can never fully become him- or herself. For Foucault, the subject has to construct his or her own universality, as the sup-port from the universal order (of tradition) has gone. Renunciation can pro-vide a route for the individual to shape his or her own universal rule to fol-low. For Lacan, renunciation produces only surplus enjoyment.[71]

CONCLUSION

In this chapter I have set out in a very preliminary way what some of the Lacanian notions of the subject and its formation might be. It might be useful to summarize several features of these notions and say something more about Lacan's idea of temporality by referring briefly to his "moment of concluding." First, the Lacanian subject is founded on a (mis)apprehension or (mis)recognition that is fundamental to the structure of subjectivity and cannot be got around. There is no final solution of wholeness or completion the subject can attain (even through psychoanalysis). The Lacanian subject is barred, radically incomplete. Second, the social or symbolic order that is brought into being with the subject and that brings the subject into being is itself incomplete or impossible; it, too, is barred.

The retroactive operation of time is significant in both these operations. The Lacanian subject never actually *is:* It only ever *will have been.* The social or symbolic order is brought into being through a rash or headlong gesture for which there is no guarantee. It is only by assuming that the social order already exists in the first place that the whole thing (subject *and* symbolic order) can come into play at all, through what Lacan calls "the moment of concluding," or "the third time":

> It is only with the third time—when by means of a gesture of precipitate identification, of an act *not covered by the big Other's guarantee,* I recognise myself in my symbolic identity mandate (as a communist, an American, a democrat . . .)—that the dimension of the big Other becomes operative. The big Other is not "always-already here" ready to provide cover for my decision: I do not merely fill in, occupy, a preordained place which awaits me in the symbolic structure—on the contrary, it is the very subjective act of recognition which, by means of its precipitate character, *establishes* the big Other *qua* atemporal-synchronous structural order.[72]

The other moments in Lacan's three moments of logical time are the instant of gaze and the time for understanding, where the subject puts him- or herself in the place of the other at the level of the imaginary.[73] Without the moment of concluding, where the subject takes an action that assumes that it is linked to other subjects through a symbolic order, neither subject positions nor symbolic order would be established: "If we simply wait for a symbolic place to be allocated to us, we will never live to see it. . . . We 'become what we are' by means of a precipitate subjective gesture."[74]

Both the lack or antagonism in the subject and in the social order are concealed, and this is where fantasy comes in. The role of politics and the political can be seen: The authority of the master signifier both *produces* the subject and the symbolic field through a retroactive operation that inscribes meaning and halts the sliding of the signifier, and *conceals* that operation, depoliticizing it and making the social order appear as "always already" preexisting. In the next chapter I turn to a discussion of ideology that draws on these notions and elaborates their implications for our understandings of the political.

NOTES

1. There are of course numerous debates around the Marxist concept of ideology. See Chapter 6 for further discussion.

2. See, for example, Michel Foucault, *Power/Knowledge: Selected Interviews and Other Writings, 1972–1977,* trans. Colin Gordon (Brighton: Harvester, 1980).

3. Michel Foucault, *The History of Sexuality,* vol. 2: *The Use of Pleasure,* trans. Robert Hurley (Harmondsworth, UK: Penguin, 1992); vol. 3: *The Care of the Self,* trans. Robert Hurley (Harmondsworth, UK: Penguin, 1990).

4. Stuart Hall, "The Question of Cultural Identity," in *Modernity and Its Futures,* ed. Stuart Hall, David Held, and Tony McGrew (London: Polity, in association with the Open University, 1992), 273–325.

5. Ernesto Laclau and Chantal Mouffe, *Hegemony and Socialist Strategy: Towards a Radical Democratic Politics* (London: Verso, 1985). For Žižek's comments on this work, see Slavoj Žižek, "Beyond Discourse Analysis," in *New Reflections on the Revolution of Our Time,* ed. Ernesto Laclau (London: Verso, 1990), 249–260. These comments are also discussed in Chapter 7.

6. I shall not be attempting to give a general overview of Lacan's work. There are a number of books that do this, including two by Žižek himself: *Looking Awry: An Introduction to Jacques Lacan Through Popular Culture* (Cambridge, MA: MIT Press, 1991); and *Enjoy Your Symptom: Jacques Lacan in Hollywood and Out* (New York: Routledge, 1992). See Joël Dor, *Introduction to the Reading of Lacan: The Unconscious Structured Like a Language,* ed. Judith Feher Gurewich, trans. Susan Fairfield (Northvale, NJ: Jason Aronson, 1997); Bruce Fink, *The Lacanian Subject: Between Language and Jouissance* (Princeton, NJ: Princeton University Press, 1995); Bruce Fink, *A Clinical Introduction to Lacanian Psychoanalysis: Theory and Technique* (Cambridge: Harvard University Press, 1997); Elizabeth Grosz, *Jacques Lacan: A Feminist Introduction* (London: Routledge, 1990). For a reading guide to *Écrits,* see John P. Muller and William J. Richardson, *Lacan and Language: A Reader's Guide to Écrits* (New York: International Universities Press, 1982). My interpretation of Lacan closely follows Žižek's work.

7. This discussion draws on Malcolm Bowie, *Lacan* (London: Fontana, 1991), particularly his chronology, 204–213.

8. Jacques Lacan, *Écrits: A Selection,* trans. Alan Sheridan (London: Routledge, 1980), 146.

9. This discussion draws on Laclau's preface to Slavoj Žižek, *The Sublime Object of Ideology* (London: Verso, 1989).

10. Žižek's publications in English since 1989 include (in addition to the two introductions to Lacan mentioned above, several edited books and numerous essays): Žižek, *Sublime Object of Ideology,* Slavoj Žižek, *For They Know Not What They Do: Enjoyment as a Political Factor* (London: Verso, 1991); Slavoj Žižek, *Tarrying with the Negative: Kant, Hegel and the Critique of Ideology* (Durham, NC: Duke University Press, 1993); Slavoj Žižek, *The Metastases of Enjoyment: Six Essays on Women and Causality* (London: Verso, 1994); Slavoj Žižek, *The Indivisible Remainder: An Essay on Schelling and Related Matters* (London: Verso, 1996); Slavoj Žižek, *The Plague of Fantasies* (London: Verso, 1997). A collection of his writings has been published in *The Žižek Reader,* ed. Elizabeth Wright and Edmond Wright (Oxford: Blackwell, 1999).

11. Examples include Judith Butler, "Arguing with the Real," in *Bodies That Matter: On the Discursive Limits of 'Sex'* (London: Routledge, 1993), 187–222;

Peter Dews, "The Tremor of Reflection: Slavoj Žižek's Lacanian Dialectics," *Radical Philosophy,* 72 (1995): 17–29. For an overview and two interviews, see Slavoj Žižek and Renata Salecl, "Lacan in Slovenia," and Slavoj Žižek, "Postscript," in *A Critical Sense: Interviews with Intellectuals,* ed. Peter Osborne (London: Routledge, 1996), 21–46. For a discussion of his popular intellectual impact, see Jenny Madden and Ben Seymour, "Terrible Old Stalinist with the Answer to Life, the Universe and Everything," *Real Life, Independent on Sunday,* 21 June 1998. See also Robert Miklitsch, "'Going Through the Fantasy': Screening Slavoj Žižek," *South Atlantic Quarterly,* 97, 2 (Spring 1998): 476–507 (special issue entitled *Psycho-Marxism: Marxism and Psychoanalysis Late in the Twentieth Century*).

12. Dews, "Tremor of Reflection," 18.

13. Žižek, *Sublime Object,* 4

14. Ibid., 5.

15. Ibid.

16. Bice Benvenuto and Roger Kennedy, *The Works of Jacques Lacan: An Introduction* (London: Free Association Books, 1986), 50.

17. Other schools of Freudianism—the American school of ego psychology, for example—do retain some concept of a unifying "self" in the ego.

18. Lacan, *Écrits,* 1.

19. As Muller and Richardson put it, "the image is a form that in-forms the subject, [gives form to] and makes possible the process of identification with it" (Muller and Richardson, *Lacan and Language,* 28).

20. Lacan, *Écrits,* 2.

21. Ibid., 4.

22. Ibid.

23. Muller and Richardson, *Lacan and Language,* 30–31.

24. Lacan, *Écrits,* 1.

25. Ibid., 5.

26. Benvenuto and Kennedy, *Lacan,* 58.

27. Lacan, *Écrits,* 22.

28. Ibid., 6. Note that "Other" is capitalized when it refers to "the symbolic order."

29. This was the aim of the American school of ego psychology, which contrasted strongly with the Lacanian school.

30. Benvenuto and Kennedy, *Lacan,* 61.

31. Lacan, *Écrits,* 297.

32. Ibid., 298.

33. Ibid.

34. Ibid.

35. Details of this and the subsequent graphs are discussed in Žižek, *The Sublime Object,* as well as Muller and Richardson, *Lacan and Language.* I do not elaborate on them here but simply draw a number of points pertinent to Žižek's analysis of ideology. I include the graphs because they give an indication of the spatiotemporal relationships that are difficult to convey verbally.

36. Ferdinand de Saussure, *Course in General Linguistics,* trans. Wade Baskin (New York: McGraw-Hill, 1966), 112.

37. Žižek, *Sublime Object,* 101.

38. Ibid., 102.

39. Ibid.

40. David Macey, "Introduction," in *The Four Fundamental Concepts of Psychoanalysis,* ed. Jacques Lacan (Harmondsworth, UK: Penguin, 1994), xx.

41. Lacan, *Écrits,* 86 (my emphasis).

42. Ibid., 87.

43. Ibid., 303.

44. Ibid.

45. Ernesto Laclau, "Preface," in Žižek, *Sublime Object,* xiv.

46. Žižek, *Sublime Object,* 103.

47. Lacan, *Écrits,* 306–307.

48. Žižek, *Sublime Object,* 110–111.

49. Ibid., 111.

50. Ibid., 113.

51. The final moment of psychoanalysis is when the subject "gets rid of the question—that is, . . . accepts his being as non-justified by the big Other" (Žižek, *Sublime Object,* 113). The question, "Why me?" disappears.

52. Žižek, *Sublime Object,* 114–115.

53. Ibid., 122.

54. The triad of the imaginary, the symbolic, and the real is discussed in more detail in Chapter 6.

55. Žižek, *Sublime Object,* 122.

56. Ibid., 123.

57. Ibid., 87.

58. As I noted in Chapter 2, the word "articulation" has the meaning here of "linking"—in the manner of an articulated lorry, as Hall puts it. Hall chooses this word in his discussions of ideology because of its dual meanings of "saying" and "linking." Saussure discusses the term in *Course,* 10.

59. Žižek, *Sublime Object,* 87.

60. Ibid., 92.

61. Ibid., 95.

62. Ibid., 95–96.

63. Ibid., 98.

64. Žižek, *Enjoy Your Symptom,* 103. This is similar to the violence of the founding "decision" in Derrida. For the role of the master signifier and a discussion of its relation to the Derridean notion of decision, see ibid., 102–103.

65. Žižek also makes contrasts with the deconstructivist view of identity. Deconstruction sees identity or "presence" as impossible in the case of opposites, which are constituted by an "outside," a supplement. These dichotomies are viewed within deconstruction, Žižek claims, as a paradoxical sort of identity. For Lacan, identity itself is nothing but a name for this "supplementary feature which 'sticks out' and suspends the essential quality of the domain whose identity it constitutes"; ibid., 89.

66. Žižek, *Sublime Object,* 100.

67. Žižek, *Enjoy Your Symptom,* 39.

68. Žižek, *Sublime Object,* 174.

69. Ibid., 175.

70. Ibid., 181.

71. Žižek, *Enjoy Your Symptom,* 179.

72. Žižek, *Indivisible Remainder,* 136

73. At the level of the imaginary (the second moment) we have a relation with the other. The relation with the big Other, the social order, takes place at the level of the symbolic.

74. Žižek, *Indivisible Remainder,* 135.

6

Ideology and Reality in Žižek

R. B. J. Walker describes the concept of ideology as "a notable and telling absence from almost all theories of international relations except as a simple descriptive synonym for 'doctrine.'"[1] The use of the term "ideology" to refer almost exclusively to political ideologies, the so-called grand ideologies, has meant that theoretical work in international relations and political theory has tended to ignore the extensive debates centered around theories of ideology in other disciplines. A recent review of textbooks on political ideologies, each of which has an introductory chapter on the nature of ideology and the history of ideology as a concept, argues that "the conception of ideology that emerges . . . restricts ideology to the major political doctrines, whilst to varying degrees, recognising that within these doctrines there are internal inconsistencies."[2] In view of the extensive work on ideology in other parts of social theory, this is an extremely limited approach, and one that ignores whole areas of debate. In particular, it does not problematize the role of the subject in relation to ideology. Individuals are seen as the authors of ideas and ideology and as being able to choose more or less freely among different ideological perspectives. There is no account of "how ideology operates on individuals and the relationship between ideology, power, language and subjectivity."[3] It is exactly these neglected aspects, which also concern how notions of ideology and the subject are linked with the political and with depoliticization, that are central to my discussion in this chapter.

The concept of ideology is perceived as awkward, not only because of the predominance of its use as a synonym for "doctrine," as I have already mentioned. Some of the reluctance to use the concept relates to its perceived links with positivism, and in particular with Marxist theory, where it has implications of false consciousness or delusion. Walker takes up this debate. He sees the problem of ideology as "rooted in the underlying problematic of identity and difference."[4] For structuralism and positivistic science, which Walker portrays as taking the position of the "one," of identity, the "difference" of the historical world of change and plurality is judged illusory. It is the abstraction of universal laws that is the "real." For the historicist, the claim to the possibility of universality is itself to be challenged: The general laws of Enlightenment science or Marxism are the object of criticism. These universal laws are themselves no more than the product of a particular (in time and place) understanding of the world. Their universality is illusory or ideological. So for Walker the ideology critique is enmeshed in the tension he sees in modern social and political theory between universalist explanations and historicist understandings.[5] But he locates poststructuralism *outside* this problematic: "For poststructuralists, of course, the real problem is the prior framework in which truth and illusion are assumed to guarantee each other."[6]

If this is the case, then why should we cling to a notion like ideology, with "such obviously outdated epistemological implications (the relationship of 'representation' between thought and reality, etc.)?"[7] The concept of "discourse," though apparently more at home in a so-called postmodern epistemology, shares these problems. The extradiscursive, like the extraideological, is problematic. As we saw in Chapter 3, Foucault considered this issue at length in *The Archaeology of Knowledge*.[8] Others are happy to conclude that there is nothing outside discourse—Laclau and Mouffe, for example, whose work I discuss in Chapter 7, take this stance.[9]

The notion of ideology is a key concept in the question of the political and depoliticization because of the way it interweaves the social or political with subjectivity and knowledge. Ideology is not concerned solely with truth and illusion but with notions of how games of truth relate to power; in this it does not assume the subject but problematizes it. Whether ideology is seen as false consciousness or as inevitable and all-pervasive, it involves the political. For ideology, Žižek argues, what matters is not the content but the way the content relates to the subject. Something is ideological once the content produces or sustains a relation of domination, power, or exploitation. Such relations have been called unavoidable in the constitution of subjectivity.

The many different notions of "ideology" can be explored using a schema that Žižek proposes, based on Hegel's three moments of religion: doctrine, belief, and ritual.[10] These three moments can be used as axes around which to place the many notions of ideology synchronously. This gives us, first, ideology as a complex of ideas (as doctrine: theories, convictions, beliefs, argumentative procedures); second, ideology as an external, material entity (materialized in social institutions, architecture, legal systems); and finally and most elusive, the spontaneous ideology at work at the heart of what we call social reality.

We could take "liberalism" as an example of how these three categories work. Liberalism is a doctrine (developed in the writings of political philosophers and economists from John Locke to Friedrich Hayek) materialized in rituals and apparatuses (the free press, elections, the market, etc.) and active in the spontaneous experience of subjects (as free individuals, making choices, taking part in exchange, etc.). It is of course debatable whether it is appropriate to use the term "ideology" in all these cases. Theorists differ on this. And even the same theorists use the term "ideology" differently at various stages of their work. Marx, for example, ceases to use "ideology" after his *Critique of Political Economy,* moving to the term "fetishism" for the spontaneous ideology inherent in social reality.[11] Post-Marxism, too, abandoned the concept (for example, between Laclau's *Politics and Ideology* in 1977 and Laclau and Mouffe's *Hegemony and Socialist Strategy* in 1985).[12] Žižek, in contrast, argues strongly for continuing to use the notion.

At each stage what appears to be a stepping out of ideology is itself an ideological position. At the level of ideology as doctrine, we have first of all the stand of Enlightenment rationality, epitomized by Jürgen Habermas, that ideology is an illusory, distorted notion of reality. For discourse analysis, this very notion—that access to reality unbiased by any discursive devices or conjunctions with power is possible, and that we can distinguish between this truth and distortion—is itself ideological. That is, what Habermas perceives as the step out of ideology is here perceived as ideology par excellence: "The 'zero level' of ideology consists in (mis)perceiving a discursive formation as an extra-discursive fact."[13]

At the level of ideology as externality, again we have regression into ideology at the very point at which we appear to step out of it: Foucault's theories of micropower come apart when they attempt to account for the formation of the state from these local micropowers. For Foucault, power inscribes itself into the body directly, bypassing ideology. Disciplinary procedures are Foucault's equivalent of Althusser's ISAs, but for Žižek abandoning the problematic of ideology is the fatal weakness in Foucault's theory.

Theories that look at the externalization of ideology in practices allow us to account for the effectivity of ideologies that are not taken seriously even by their promoters, such as fascism. This also happens when we look at the spontaneous ideology at work in the heart of what we call social reality itself. The argument that we no longer live in an age of ideology claims, for example, that ideologies such as Protestantism are no longer widespread or that in the age of media proliferation none of us acts on our beliefs anymore. The system and its reproduction, the argument goes, bypass ideology and rely more on economic coercion and state regulations. It is these, not a common ideology or belief, that guarantee social cohesion and stability.

Again, however, this very stepping outside of ideology can be seen as another reversal: These allegedly extraideological mechanisms are part of an "obscure domain" in which reality is indistinguishable from ideology.[14] Žižek argues that these mechanisms of social control materialize propositions or beliefs that are inherently ideological and that even the form of consciousness that fits late capitalist, postideological society also remains ideological. There is an "elusive network of implicit, quasi-'spontaneous' presuppositions and attitudes that form an irreducible moment of the reproduction of 'non-ideological' (economic, legal, political, sexual . . .) practices."[15] Yet again, having seemingly stepped outside ideology, we remain thoroughly caught in the ideological.[16]

Ideology thus remains an important notion because of the way it interweaves the political with subjectivity and notions of truth. At each of the three moments of ideology—doctrine, practice, and belief—it is when we appear to step outside ideology that we remain caught within it. We can now begin to explore in more detail how notions of the ideological are linked with and arise from a problematization of the subject.

SOCIAL FANTASY

As we saw in the previous chapter, the upper level of the graph of desire (Figure 5.5) can be read as involving a dimension "beyond interpellation." But it is this upper level that is left out, according to Žižek, from theories of ideology that follow the Althusserian approach to interpellation. Poststructuralism tries to move beyond interpellation by looking at the plurality and dispersion of the signifying process: As we saw in the discussion of Foucault in Chapter 3, this can lead to a rejection of the dimension of "ideology." But this is not what is important: Where we should be looking, Žižek argues, is at "the square of desire, fantasy, lack in the Other and drive pulsating around some unbearable surplus-enjoyment."[17]

Žižek claims that to take account of this we need to look beyond the analysis of ideology as discourse—the way discursive mechanisms constitute the field of ideological meaning—which would be the approach of Gramsci or Hall, or indeed of Laclau and Mouffe. We need to incorporate a second strand in our analysis of ideology, to give two complementary procedures of the "criticism of ideology":

> (1) one is discursive, the "symptomal reading" of the ideological text bringing about the "deconstruction" of the spontaneous experience of its meaning—that is, demonstrating how a given ideological field is a result of a montage of heterogeneous "floating signifiers," of their totalisation through the intervention of certain "nodal points";
>
> (2) the other aims at extracting the kernel of enjoyment, at articulating the way in which—beyond the field of meaning but at the same time

internal to it—an ideology implies, manipulates, produces a pre-ideological enjoyment structured in fantasy.[18]

So Žižek is proposing a second strand—following an analysis of discourse through Laclau and Mouffe's (Gramscian/deconstructive) approach—a Lacanian analysis of enjoyment. This means supplementing Althusser's use of Lacan's notion of interpellation with a Lacanian notion at another level, that of enjoyment. The level of discourse analysis involves articulating aspects such as symbolic overdetermination, displacement, associations, and condensation and undoing them to uncover their meaning. This takes interpretation. But this does not explain how a particular ideology captures our desire. To do this, we need to explore how it enters the fantasy framework structuring our enjoyment. But fantasy is not to be interpreted like discourse; Žižek believes fantasy is to be "traversed": "All we have to do is to experience how there is nothing 'behind' it, and how fantasy masks precisely this 'nothing.'"[19]

This nothing is, however, crucial:

It is through the mediation of this "nothing" that the subject constitutes himself in the very act of his misrecognition. The illusion that there is something hidden behind the curtain is thus a reflexive one: what is hidden behind the appearance is the possibility of this very illusion—behind the curtain is the fact that the subject thinks something must be behind it. The illusion, albeit "false," is effectively located in the empty place behind the curtain—the illusion has opened a place where it is possible, an empty space that it fills out—where the "illusory reality," reduplicating the external, factual reality, could find its proper place.[20]

For Žižek, the notion of social fantasy is a counterpart to Laclau and Mouffe's notion of social antagonism: Every society is structured around a constitutive impossibility or antagonism.[21] Ideology or social fantasy masks this antagonism. The totalitarian project already knows its impossibility, and this knowledge is included in its edifice. In fascism, for example, the whole ideology "is structured as a struggle against the element which holds the place of the immanent impossibility of the very Fascist project: the 'Jew.'"[22] This then gives a third procedure of the "criticism of ideology," supplementing the ones given above: "(3) to detect, in a given ideological edifice, the element which represents within it its own impossibility."[23]

But—and this is crucial—at this point Žižek elaborates what he means by "going through the fantasy." It is in this process that we "identify with the symptom," that is, recognize that in the properties attributed to the symptom is the necessary product of our social system itself. Lacan claims that it was Marx who invented the symptom. Žižek explains the link:

Marx's great achievement was to demonstrate how all phenomena which
appear to everyday bourgeois consciousness as simple deviations, contingent deformations and degenerations of the "normal" functioning of
society (economic crises, wars, and so on), and as such abolishable
through amelioration of the system, are necessary products of the system
itself—the points at which "truth," the immanent antagonistic character
of the system, erupts. To identify with the "symptom" means to recognise
in the "excesses," in the disruptions of the "normal" way of things, the
key offering us access to [the system's] true functioning. This is similar
to Freud's view that the keys to the functioning of the human mind were
dreams, slips of the tongue, and similar "abnormal" phenomena.[24]

Žižek also explores what "identifying with the symptom" might mean
in the context of (what we call) crises. He elaborates on this process when
he discusses reaction to the persecution of the Jews. A whole series of re-
actions are possible: ignoring it; treating it as something that does not concern us, some sort of primitive "ritual"; or showing "sincere compassion"
for the victims. All these "allow us to evade the fact that the persecution of
Jews pertains to a certain repressed truth of our civilisation."[25] We attain
an authentic attitude only when we realize that in a real sense "we are all
Jews." In other words,

> By means of such an identification with the (social) symptom, we tra-
> verse and subvert the fantasy frame that determines the field of social
> meaning, the ideological self-understanding of a particular society, i.e.,
> the frame within which, precisely, the "symptom" appears as some alien,
> disturbing intrusion, and not as the point of eruption of the otherwise hid-
> den truth of the existing social order.[26]

The symptom, the crisis, is not external, "other" to the social order. It is
the point within that particular order where its "truth" erupts.

If the emergency, the disaster, the holocaust is not external to the social order but its symptom, in a parallel way the foreigner, the outcast, the
madman in Foucault, the victim or the scapegoat is not outside either but
within. Julia Kristeva discusses how the stranger or the foreigner is not external, not "other," "neither the romantic victim of our clannish indolence
nor the intruder responsible for all the ills of the polis."[27] It is for Kristeva
only by recognition of the stranger "within ourselves" or, as Žižek might
put it, acknowledgment of our symptom, that hatred of the foreigner, the
other can be overcome: .

> Strangely, the foreigner lives within us: he is the hidden face of our iden-
> tity, the space that wrecks our abode, the time in which understanding and
> affinity founder. . . . A symptom that precisely turns "we" into a problem,
> perhaps makes it impossible, the foreigner comes in when the conscious-
> ness of my difference arises, and he disappears when we all acknowledge
> ourselves as foreigners, unamenable to bonds and communities.[28]

SOCIAL REALITY

Žižek uses "real," "reality," and "Real" with a variety of meanings, exploiting a certain slippage in these terms. The Lacanian real is similarly elusive and resistant to being pinned down. This part of the chapter elaborates on these notions a little before going on to discuss "reality" in relation to Žižek's concept of ideology.

Lacan's theory moved through a variety of uses of the notion of the "real." Initially, as part of the triumvirate real-symbolic-imaginary, the "real" was brute reality, reality before symbolization. Later the real became more like what Lacan had originally called the "Imaginary." This gives the real in Lacan what Žižek calls a paradoxical character:

> [It] is *real*—it is a hard core resisting symbolisation, but . . . it does not matter if it has had a place, if it has "really occurred" in so-called reality; the point is simply that it produces a series of structural effects (displacements, repetitions, and so on). The Real is an entity which must be constructed afterwards so that we can account for the distortions of the symbolic structure.[29]

Laclau and Mouffe's concept of "antagonism" demonstrates, according to Žižek, this logic of the real in its relevance for the social-ideological field. "Antagonism" as such does not exist, but it prevents closure of the social field, the totalization that is always already impossible.[30] This prohibition of the impossible attests to the presence of the real. Žižek cites Ludwig Wittgenstein's "Whereof one cannot speak, thereof one must be silent" as another example of an impossible prohibition testifying to the presence of the real. The Lacanian real is "an entity which, although it does not exist (in the sense of 'really existing,' taking place in reality), has a series of properties"[31] and can produce certain effects. In the end, "the Real is nothing but [the] impossibility of its inscription: the Real is not a transcendent positive entity, persisting somewhere beyond the symbolic order like a hard kernel inaccessible to it. . . . In itself it is nothing at all, just a void, an emptiness in a symbolic structure marking some central impossibility."[32]

Lacan argues that (what we call) external reality is constituted or posited by the subject. The self is converted into being through the emergence of the symbolic order, or symbolic fictions. Individual deeds exist only by reference to these symbolic fictions, such as the state, for example. The big Other (the symbolic order) must be presupposed. "The Fatherland, the cause for which we fight, is 'nowhere in reality' but in spite of this we cannot explain the very 'material' reality of fights and sufferings without reference to it."[33] For Žižek, "reality" is not something that is given but something of which the ontological status is secondary: "What we call '(external) reality' constitutes itself by means of a primordial act of 'rejection.'"[34] Freud saw a discord between the logic of the psyche, which operated by the "pleasure principle," and the demands of reality. Lacan (and the late Freud) sees the problem that prevented the circle of pleasure from closing as inherent to the psyche. This internal self-impediment (the real) is externalized by the subject. The external limit posited by the subject constitutes "reality."

The form of reality constituted by the symbolic order can perhaps be illustrated by looking at the example of money. We know that money, like all material objects, suffers wear in use. But we treat coins and notes as if they consisted of an immaterial substance, an "indestructible and immutable" body that persists, despite changes in the physical body. This Žižek calls the sublime material: Money is a "sublime object." What is crucial in his argument is that "the postulated existence of the sublime body depends on the symbolic order: the indestructible 'body-within-a-body' exempted from the effects of wear and tear is always sustained by the guarantee of some symbolic authority."[35] Although the use of money in the process of exchange has nothing to do with the "reality" of its material properties, it is nevertheless not a "thought abstraction" in the sense of taking place in the interior of a thinking subject. It has the form of thought, but is "external to thought itself." The thought is "always already"—there is some other scene where the thought is articulated in advance. Žižek compares this with the unconscious and relates it to the symbolic order: For Žižek, "the symbolic order is precisely such a formal order which supplements and/or disrupts the dual relationship of 'external' factual reality and 'internal' subjective experience."[36] The symbolic order (the social order) subverts the very distinction between the real object and the thought.

So money is real but not real, an abstraction but not an abstraction.[37] Its social function depends on the acceptance of a symbolic order, an acceptance that is ideological. Without ignorance of this underpinning, the function itself dissolves: Money is seen as worthless, and the exchange process collapses. "Practical" consciousness is also blind to what is going on in the exchange process—were it not, the process itself could not occur as an effective act. The exchange process is an example of "a kind of reality which is possible only on condition that the individuals partaking in it are *not* aware of its proper logic; that is a kind of reality *whose very ontological consistency implies a certain non-knowledge of its participants*— if we come to know too much, to pierce the true functioning of social reality, this reality would dissolve itself."[38] Ideology is implicated in the very processes of (what we call) social reality.

In the next section, I bring out these notions of real and reality and their implications for theorizing about ideology by looking at the contrasting views of Marx and Lacan; the chapter ends with a general discussion of the question, Is there a place for ideology critique? In Marx, ideology *conceals* social reality. It is superstructural, concealing the fundamental antagonism at the root of the capitalist system. Revolution—abolition of the system—is the solution. In Žižek's Lacanian work, ideology *enables* social reality. The ideological is not simply "false consciousness," an illusory representation of reality. "'Ideological' is a social reality whose very existence implies the non-knowledge of its participants as to its essence," or in other words, "'Ideological' is not the 'false consciousness' of a (social) being but this being itself in so far as it is supported by 'false consciousness.'"[39] Ideology lies not only in thought but also in actions. All attempts at society face a constitutive antagonism, without which no society is possible. The solution is to live with (and acknowledge) that antagonism.

Žižek stresses that ideological illusion is not located just in the "knowing" but also in the "doing"—in reality itself. Previous analyses have considered that the illusion was on the side of the knowing: People do not know what they are really doing; they have a false representation of the social reality to which they belong. But for Žižek "the illusion is not on the side of knowledge, it is already on the side of reality itself, of what the people are doing. What they do not know is that their social reality itself, their activity, is guided by an illusion."[40] People know what they are doing, but they continue to do it:

> The illusion is therefore double: it consists in overlooking the illusion which is structuring our real, effective relationship to reality. And this overlooked, unconscious illusion is what may be called *the ideological fantasy.* . . . People no longer believe in ideological truth; they do not take ideological propositions seriously. The fundamental level of ideology, however, is not of an illusion masking the real state of things but that of an (unconscious) fantasy structuring our social reality itself. . . . Even if we do not take things seriously, even if we keep an ironical distance, we are still doing them.[41]

Žižek argues that belief is externalized in social activity. In feudalism, relations between people are mystified; in capitalism, this mystification is carried by relations between things. People no longer believe (they see themselves as free, rational beings), but the things (commodities) believe for them. "What we call 'social reality' is in the last resort an ethical construction; it is supported by a certain *as if.* . . . As soon as the belief (which . . . is embodied, materialised in the effective functioning of the social field) is lost, the very texture of the social field disintegrates."[42] The answer to unbelief is to forget rational debate and instead to take part in ideological ritual, to repeat the meaningless gestures, act *as if* you already believe, and the belief will come. The correct behavior leads to actual belief before conscious belief. Žižek draws attention to the Lacanian thesis that "in the opposition between dream and reality, fantasy is on the side of reality: it is . . . the support that gives consistency to what we call 'reality.'"[43] It enables us to mask the real of our desire.

Ideology is the same:

> [It] is not a dreamlike illusion that we build to escape insupportable reality; in its basic dimension it is a fantasy-construction which serves as a support for our "reality" itself: an "illusion" which structures our effective, real social relations and thereby masks some insupportable, real, impossible kernel (conceptualised by Ernesto Laclau and Chantal Mouffe as "antagonism": a traumatic social division which cannot be symbolised). The function of ideology is not to offer us a point of escape from our reality but to offer us the social reality itself as an escape from some traumatic, real kernel.[44]

To say that the support of "reality" is fantasy, however, is not to say, "Life is a dream," "What we call reality is just an illusion," and so on.

> The Lacanian thesis is, on the contrary, that there is always a hard kernel, a leftover which persists and cannot be reduced to a universal play of illusory mirroring. . . . For Lacan, the only point at which we approach this hard kernel of the Real is indeed the dream. . . . only in the dream [do we approach] the fantasy-framework which determines our activity, our mode of acting in reality itself.[45]

In our everyday activity, we are nothing but a consciousness of the dream.

It is the same with the ideological dream. We cannot break out of the ideological dream and see reality "as it is." "The only way to break the power of our ideological dream is to confront the Real of our desire which announces itself in this dream."[46] We must confront ourselves with how we have constructed the "ideological" to escape a deadlock in our own social reality. We cannot do this by confronting the ideological with reality: "Ideology succeeds in determining the mode of our everyday experience of reality itself."[47] Thus "in the predominant Marxist perspective the ideological gaze is a *partial* gaze overlooking [that is, ignoring] the *totality* of social relations, whereas in the Lacanian perspective ideology rather designates *a totality set on effacing the traces of its own impossibility.*" Furthermore,

> From the Marxist point of view, the ideological procedure *par excellence* is that of *"false" eternalisation and/or universalisation:* a state which depends on a concrete historical conjunction appears as an eternal, universal feature of the human condition. . . . In the Lacanian perspective, we should change the terms and designate as the most "cunning" ideological procedure the very opposite of eternalisation: an *over-rapid historicisation.* . . . Over-rapid historicisation makes us blind to the real kernel which returns as the same through diverse historicisations/symbolisations.[48]

This contrast between Marxist and Lacanian approaches is summarized in Table 6.1.

If we cannot escape the ideological, if the social itself implies an ideological illusion, what place is there for a critique of ideology? And how does this relate to the political? Žižek sees no solution to the problem of the social without totalization, which involves ideological masking of its constitutive lack, or what I have called depoliticization or technologization. He asks whether it is possible instead to "tarry with the negative," to live with a constitutive antagonism. He argues that we should abandon the Marxist notion that a class antagonism lies at the root of all antagonisms and that by solving this struggle we solve all others. He extends this claim to all other "fundamental" antagonisms, like feminist fundamentalism, democratic fundamentalism, and ecological fundamentalism. It is psychoanalysis of the Lacanian type that breaks with this "essentialist logic" by affirming "the irreducible plurality of particular struggles—in other words, . . . how their articulation into a series of equivalences always depends on the radical contingency of the social-historical process: it enables us to grasp this plurality itself as a multitude of responses to the same impossible-real kernel."[49] This leads us to the opposite of the traditional Marxist view, where the solution of all particular antagonisms is seen in global revolution: Here, "every provisional, temporarily successful solution of a particular problem entails an acknowledgement of the global radical deadlock, impossibility, the acknowledgement of a fundamental antagonism."[50]

CONCLUSION

In this chapter I have shown how Žižek's psychoanalytic approach draws on and develops a Lacanian notion of subjectivity and how he elaborates

Table 6.1   Marxist and Lacanian Approaches

Marxist	Lacanian
Surplus Value	Surplus Enjoyment
Ideological gaze is a partial gaze overlooking the totality of social relations.	Ideology designates a totality set on effacing the traces of its own impossibility.
Fetish conceals the positive network of social relations.	Fetish conceals the lack around which the symbolic network is articulated.
"Ideological" procedure is that of false eternalization and/or universalization.	The most "cunning" ideological procedure is overrapid historicization.

a conception of ideology. Starting from the problematic of the constitution of the self, Žižek produces an account of the role of ideology in the constitution of social reality. His elucidation of the formation of consciousness or subjectivity sees the social as implicated in this process from the start, in contrast to accounts based on psychological or psychoanalytical approaches that begin with the construction of the individual before moving to an account of the social.

The account, as we have seen, leads to a conception of ideology distinct both from discourse analysis, which refuses to give any account of "reality," and from a theory of ideology of the "Marxist" type, which implies an unproblematic access to a nonideological reality. In fact this account is based on a challenge to the distinction between "reality" and "nonreality." Žižek claims in effect that this distinction is at the root of the ideological. He also sees the symbolic order, social reality, as subversive of it.[51]

For Žižek, the constitution of subjectivity and (what we call) social reality depends both on the rejection of an impossible-real kernel—an antagonism that is nonsymbolizable yet must be presupposed—and on the concealment of this rejection through ideological fantasy. The utopia of a complete social whole without antagonism would lead to totalitarianism. The critique of ideology must identify in a given social order elements that "point towards the system's antagonistic character and thus 'estrange' us from the self-evidence of its established identity."[52]

In the introduction to his book *Tarrying with the Negative,* Žižek describes rebels in Romania in 1989 waving the national flag, with the red star, the Communist symbol, cut out from its center, leaving nothing but a hole.[53] This epitomized the brief period of openness, a state of passage, where the old apparatus had been cast off and a new one had not yet appeared. For this brief interim, the "hole" in the symbolic order was visible. It could be seen in this symbol of the flag. Žižek sees the role of the critique of ideology as offering this type of skepticism all the time. According to Žižek,

> The duty of the critical intellectual—if, in today's "postmodern" universe, this syntagm has any meaning left—is precisely *to occupy all the time,* even when the new order . . . stabilizes itself and again renders invisible the hole as such, *the place of this hole,* i.e., to maintain a distance toward every reigning Master-Signifier. . . . The aim is precisely to "produce" the Master Signifier, that is to say, to render visible its "produced," artificial, contingent character.[54]

As we have seen, "social reality" as such requires an organizing "master signifier." The critique of ideology tries to make it impossible to conceal this, to "naturalize" or depoliticize the social structure.

This is a reason for maintaining the need for ideology critique as opposed to discourse analysis. The conclusion of discourse analysis seems to be that the only nonideological position is to renounce the very notion of extraideological reality: All we are dealing with are symbolic fictions, the plurality of discursive universes, not "reality." This is not a way out, however. Žižek maintains that "such a quick, slick 'postmodern' solution" is ideology par excellence. What he claims to offer is another way of retaining the ideology critique and a nonideological position from which to offer this critique. To remain outside ideology, *we must persist in the impossible position.* We do this by recognizing and placing ourselves within the *undecidable opposition* that, as we saw at the beginning of the chapter, lies in wait at every stage of the ideology debate.[55] We must assume an "empty place" from which ideology can be denounced: "Although no clear line of demarcation separates ideology from reality, although ideology is already at work in everything we experience as 'reality,' we must none the less maintain the tension that keeps the critique of ideology alive."[56]

Where or what is this empty place? How can we "assume" it? This is a difficult notion, which returns us to the notion of "reality" and the real in Lacan. The argument turns on the impossibility of drawing a clear line between the real and unreal, between ideological and nonideological. To try to elaborate the line Žižek takes, I begin by returning to the threefold split inherent in the concept of ideology discussed above. We saw there that at each stage of Žižek's discussion of ideology—doctrine, belief, and ritual—he identifies an opposition or split that is *undecidable,* an alternative inside-outside (Žižek later calls this same split "spontaneous"-nonspontaneous).[57]

To explain this Žižek draws a parallel between Lacanian notions of the surplus and Derridean notions of the specter.[58] The Lacanian surplus is inherent in the "mirror" relationship between spirituality and corporeality, the ideal and the real, the inside and the outside. There is a spiritual element of corporeality, and the material element of spirituality is the materialization of the spirit in the specter. In Derridean notions of the specter, the same "elusive pseudo-materiality that subverts the classical ontological oppositions of reality and illusion" is in question. If there is no reality without the specter, this means that the circle of reality cannot be closed, completed, without the spectral "supplement."

In Lacan's version what we experience as "reality" is always already symbolized, constructed, and constituted by the symbolic. But this process of symbolization always fails: There is always a surplus that resists symbolization, that remains of the real—there is always "some unsettled, unredeemed symbolic debt." Žižek argues that it is this that "returns in the guise of spectral apparitions." The specter is the part of reality that cannot be symbolized, that remains outside the attempt at complete symbolization. That "reality" is always a fiction, that "reality" is symbolically or socially constructed is a separate notion. The two notions are incompatible, Žižek holds: "Reality is never directly 'itself,' it presents itself only via its incomplete-fxailed symbolisation, and spectral apparitions emerge in this very gap that forever separates reality from the real, and on account of which reality has the character of a symbolic fiction: the specter gives body to that which escapes (the symbolically structured) reality."[59]

The performative fills this gap, too, *and ideology is in the same business of "completing" reality*. According to Žižek, it is Lacan's work that can provide the answer to this question of why there is no reality without the specter:

> The preideological "kernel" of ideology [is] the spectral apparition that fills up the hole of the real. This is what all attempts to draw a clear line . . . between "true" reality and illusion (or to ground illusion in reality) fail to take into account: if (what we experience as) "reality" is to emerge, something has to be foreclosed from it—that is to say, "reality," like truth, is, by definition, never "whole." What the specter conceals is not reality but its "primordially repressed," the irrepresentable X on whose "repression" reality itself is founded.[60]

Žižek considers this the answer to the (empty) place from which ideology critique is possible: "The very constitution of social reality involves the 'primordial repression' of an antagonism, so that the ultimate support of the critique of ideology—the extra-ideological point of reference that authorises us to denounce the content of our immediate experience as 'ideological'—is not 'reality' but the 'repressed' real of antagonism."[61]

There is in Žižek's view no solution to the antagonism that lies at the root of the social. It is constitutive, inherent in the form of the social as such. We must find a way of living with the antagonism. In this concluding section I have looked at how this solution might work, what "living with antagonism" might mean, and what the role of the intellectual might be. In the next chapter, the last, I return to the question of how this can inform a discussion of "the political" and ethics, and explore how a succession of repoliticizations might be possible.

NOTES

1. R. B. J. Walker, *Inside/Outside: International Relations as Political Theory* (Cambridge: Cambridge University Press, 1993), 115.

2. Rose Gann, "The Limits of Textbook Ideology," *Politics*, 15, 2 (1995): 129.

3. Ibid., 131–132.

4. Walker, *Inside/Outside*, 115.

5. For an extended discussion of this tension in the context of international relations theory, see Martin Hollis and Steve Smith, *Explaining and Understanding International Relations* (Oxford: Oxford University Press, 1990).

6. Walker, *Inside/Outside,* 115.

7. Slavoj Žižek, "The Spectre of Ideology," in *Mapping Ideology,* ed. Slavoj Žižek (London: Verso, 1994), 3. Žižek goes on to argue that we need to detach ideology from its association with ideas of illusion. Instead he claims that "one of the tasks of the 'post-modern' critique of ideology [is] to designate the elements within an existing social order which . . . point towards the system's antagonistic character, and thus 'estrange' us to the self-evidence of its established identity" (ibid., 7).

8. Michel Foucault, *The Archaeology of Knowledge,* trans. A. M. Sheridan Smith (London: Routledge, 1989).

9. The term "discourse" is also used as a loose synonym for "text" or for "language" in its narrow, literal sense, which does not help.

10. Žižek, "Spectre of Ideology," 9.

11. Karl Marx, "Preface to 'A Critique of Political Economy,'" in *Karl Marx: Selected Writings,* ed. David McLellan (Oxford: Oxford University Press, 1977), 388–391.

12. Ernesto Laclau, *Politics and Ideology in Marxist Theory* (Oxford: Blackwell, 1979); and Ernesto Laclau and Chantal Mouffe, *Hegemony and Socialist Strategy: Towards a Radical Democratic Politics* (London: Verso, 1985).

13. Žižek, "Spectre of Ideology," 10.

14. Ibid.

15. Ibid., 15.

16. The question whether this does not make ideology altogether too all-embracing remains.

17. Žižek, *Sublime Object,* 124.

18. Ibid., 125.

19. Ibid., 126.

20. Ibid., 193.

21. Laclau and Mouffe's definition of an ideological discourse as one where there is no recognition of an outside or an other that constitutes that discourse is interesting here. David Howarth, "Discourse Theory," in *Theory and Methods in Political Science,* ed. David Marsh and Gerry Stoker (London: Macmillan, 1995), 115–133.

22. Žižek, *Sublime Object,* 127.

23. Ibid.

24. Ibid. 128. To Žižek's list of social "disruptions"—economic crises, wars, and so on—we could, of course, add famines. Elsewhere I have explored the implications of this interpretation and examined whether "famines" have been replaced as "disruptions" in the post–cold war world order by the questions of "humanitarian intervention" (Jenny Edkins, *Famines and Modernity: Pictures of Hunger, Concepts of Famine, Practices of Aid* [Minneapolis: University of Minnesota Press, forthcoming]).

25. Žižek, *Looking Awry: An Introduction to Jacques Lacan Through Popular Culture* (Cambridge, MA: MIT Press, 1991), 140.

26. Ibid.

27. Julia Kristeva, *Strangers to Ourselves,* trans. Leon S. Roudiez (New York: Columbia University Press, 1991), 1.

28. Ibid.

29. Žižek, *Sublime Object,* 162.

30. Žižek argues that the Marxian concept of "class struggle" is an example of a notion designed to cover this "gap" in the social by designating the antagonism

that prevents the social from constituting itself as a whole. Class struggle exists so that social phenomena can be described as attempts to efface the rift of class antagonism. Society is held together by the very notion that prevents its constitution as a harmonious whole. The absence of struggle is already a form of struggle: the victory of one of the sides in the struggle. The Marxian notion of class struggle is "real" in the Lacanian sense: It is the Lacanian "real," a hitch, an impediment that gives rise to new symbolizations in an attempt to get around it but that also means that these endeavors do not work.

31. Žižek, *Sublime Object,* 163.

32. Ibid., 173.

33. Slavoj Žižek, *Enjoy Your Symptom: Jacques Lacan in Hollywood and Out* (New York: Routledge, 1992), 52.

34. Ibid., 49.

35. Žižek, *Sublime Object,* 18–19.

36. Ibid., 19.

37. Like the specter, as we shall see in the concluding section.

38. Žižek, *Sublime Object,* 21.

39. Ibid.

40. Ibid., 32.

41. Ibid., 32–33.

42. Ibid., 36.

43. Ibid., 44.

44. Ibid., 45.

45. Ibid., 47.

46. Ibid., 48.

47. Ibid., 49.

48. Ibid., 49–50.

49. Ibid., 4.

50. Ibid., 6.

51. Judith Butler develops a similar critique in her discussions of the constitution of "materiality." Judith Butler, *Bodies That Matter: On the Discursive Limits of 'Sex'* (London: Routledge, 1993), chapter 1.

52. Slavoj Žižek, *Tarrying with the Negative: Kant, Hegel and the Critique of Ideology* (Durham, NC: Duke University Press, 1993), 231.

53. A similar scene occurred in the streets of Belgrade in demonstrations in the early weeks of 1997, when the opposition removed the red partisan star from the Serbian flag.

54. Žižek, *Tarrying,* 2.

55. This also, of course, evokes the discussion of the undecidable in the previous chapter.

56. Žižek, "Spectre of Ideology," 17.

57. This tension between inside and outside, between "spontaneous" and "imposed,"

> introduces a kind of reflective distance into the very heart of the notion of ideology: ideology is always, by definition, "ideology of ideology."
> . . . There is no ideology that does not assert itself by means of delimiting itself from another "mere ideology." An individual subjected to ideology can never say for himself "I am in ideology," he always requires another corpus of doxa in order to distinguish his own "true" position from it. (Ibid., 19–20)

58. Lacan's approach to spectrality can be distinguished from Derrida's view, Žižek argues. For Derrida, Marx's original promise of justice as "spectral Otherness" was messianic: It related only to the *avenir,* the yet-to-come. The totalitarian turn of Marxism came with the "ontologisation of the specter," the withdrawal from spectrality. The spectral promise was translated into a positive ontological project, which related to the simple *futur,* the what-will-be. For Lacan, there is more to spectrality than this: "Spectre as such always bears witness to a retreat, a withdrawal" (Žižek "Spectre of Ideology," 27). According to Žižek, the Lacanian specter already emerges out of a retreat from a moment of freedom, freedom from the symbolic reality in which we are, usually, embedded.

59. Ibid., 21.

60. Ibid.

61. Ibid., 25.

7

The Political
and Repoliticization

This chapter begins with an examination of two approaches often described as "post-Marxist," both of which argue for the specificity of the political: the work of Stuart Hall and that of Ernesto Laclau and Chantal Mouffe. Hall's work provides an interesting illustration of how an analysis of the political itself functions as a political intervention. His call to the left in Britain is a call for a reimagining of the social order—a re-visioning of the political—and his analysis of racial politics in the 1970s shows how a political issue, "race," is depoliticized and securitized. Hall's more recent work has examined ethnicity and race as political identities, and this move is a significant one. Concepts of time, postcolonialism, and subjectivity in Homi Bhabha's work provide an astute analysis of how Western politics is constituted. In these and other texts that form part of postcolonial studies, the discussions of subjectivity that we have examined within the discourse of poststructuralism gain a political immediacy and purchase that may not be apparent elsewhere.

Laclau and Mouffe's book *Hegemony and Socialist Strategy* uses Foucauldian notions of discourse and makes an important contribution to the theorization of the political, particularly, as Žižek has noted, through its analysis of antagonism. My interest here is, first, to set out this contribution and criticisms of it and, second, to indicate the extent to which the notion of hegemony used by Laclau and Mouffe parallels the idea of depoliticization or technologization I have developed in this book. Laclau and Mouffe have responded to Žižek's criticisms and to his work on ideology (discussed in the previous chapter) by bringing into their later work on the political a more psychoanalytic model of the subject and subjectivity. I examined some of this work in Chapter 1, and I return to it here prior to my concluding discussion of "the political."

In Chapter 1 I discussed at length the distinction between "politics" as one domain of the social and "the political" as a moment when the founding principle of the social order is in abeyance. In this view, the political represents the moment of openness or undecidability, when a new social order is on the point of establishment, when its limits are being contested. Politics, in contrast, is what takes place once the new order is institutionalized. It is the debate that occurs *within* the limits set by that order. In an important sense, then, the political could be described as a moment that depoliticizes: The most intensely political moment, the moment of decision, itself brings about the forgetting of the political that installs politics.

As a moment, this foundational instant cannot be effective without being forgotten, without erasing its own traces. What Žižek calls "the 'political' dimension" can be seen then as "*doubly inscribed:* it is a moment of the social Whole, one among its sub-systems, *and* the very terrain in which the fate of the Whole is decided."[1] The moment of the political, what we have seen Derrida call "decision," is a moment of ethicopolitical responsibility; what takes place thereafter is a return to calculability within a delimited context of a specific social world. As Derrida puts it, "There is no responsibility, no ethicopolitical decision, that must not pass through the proofs of the incalculable or the undecidable. Otherwise everything would be reducible to calculation, program, causality, and at best, 'hypothetical imperative.'"[2]

In concluding this book, I examine how the notion of the political or the decision can be linked with the Lacanian concept of the act, and how this implicates the subject. I consider Žižek's argument that "politics" has an ideological function as a metaphor or master signifier that conceals a lack in the social order—or to use our terminology, the depoliticization of the social order. This recalls the argument that sovereignty performs this same function in contemporary politics. Finally, I return to ethicopolitical implications to explore Žižek's "ethics of the real" as a parallel to the ethics of responsibility that has been derived from Derrida.

THE SPECIFICITY OF THE POLITICAL

Hall's work has affinities with and draws on many of the approaches examined in this book, although he would hesitate to label it "poststructuralist" and would certainly contest the notions of play and multiplicity many ascribe to it.[3] He regards himself as a poststructuralist and a post-Marxist only in the sense that Marxism and structuralism are "the two discourses [he] feels most constantly engaged with."[4] His work is occupied with several of the areas I have covered here, from an interest in the 1970s and 1980s in ideology to a concern with identity, ethnicity, and the subject, particularly in relation to postcolonialism, nationalism, and cultural studies.[5]

Hall's work takes a Gramscian line, drawing as well on Althusser in developing a theorization of ideological struggle in terms of the articulation

and rearticulation of elements. Hall describes this as "a way of understanding how ideological elements come, under certain conditions, to co-
here together within a discourse, and a way of asking how they do or do
not become articulated, at specific conjunctures, to certain political subjects."[6] The notion of articulation is developed in Laclau's book *Politics
and Ideology in Marxist Theory*.[7] The work on ideology took place while
Hall was part of the collective at the Centre for Contemporary Cultural
Studies at the University of Birmingham. This research was very much inspired by V. N. Vološinov's notion of the multiaccentual character of the
sign, and the consequent possibility of shifting and play—articulation and
rearticulation.[8] The parallel between this "logic" of ideology and the logic
of dream work in Freud was clear, as was the connection with power and
the political: "Vološinov's account counterposed the existence of cultural
power through the imposition of the norm in an attempt to freeze and fix
meaning in language to the constant eruption of new meanings, the fluidity
of heteroglossia, and the way meaning's inherent instability and heterogeneity dislocated and displaced language's apparently 'finished' character."[9]

Hall's work has always engaged directly with politics and the political. He is well known outside academia for his writings on Thatcherism
in the late 1970s and the 1980s (especially "The Great Moving Right
Show," first published in *Marxism Today* in 1978) and has recently written
on New Labour in the 1990s (in an article entitled "The Great Moving
Nowhere Show").[10] His major study of racism in Britain is less well
known, although it provides another demonstration and a working through
of his analysis of the political.[11]

In his investigation of Thatcherism, Hall defends an approach that
concentrates on "the specificity of the political." He argues that the "crisis of the left" in British politics in the 1980s arose in part from a neglect
of this aspect. He analyzes the political in terms of attempts at hegemony,
which he defines in a Gramscian way as

> the struggle to contest and dis-organise an existing political formation;
> the taking of the "leading position" (on however a minority a basis) over
> a number of different spheres of society at once—economy, civil society,
> intellectual and moral life, culture; the conduct of a wide and differenti-
> ated type of struggle; the winning of a strategic measure of popular con-
> sent; and, thus, the securing of a social authority sufficiently deep to con-
> form society into a new historical project.[12]

Significant for our discussions in this chapter, hegemony he sees as "always contested, always trying to secure itself, always 'in process.'"[13]
Hegemony is not something that is won once and for all but something that
can at best be momentarily secured.

In a similar way, the political is not a question of conflict between preexisting classes or other groupings whose interests can be presumed but

rather a question of the struggle to form new (and always precarious) coalitions of power. Hall insists in particular that the conventional wisdom of Marxist thought, which saw a simple correspondence between the economic and the political, has ended. Classes are no longer seen as constituted at the economic level and transposed directly to the political; instead, "political and ideological questions [must] be addressed in their full specificity, without reduction."[14]

What Thatcherism understood fully, and what the left has still to learn, according to Hall, is how the process of realignment works and how it can be used to win hegemony for a new political project. There is more to it than that, though. Whereas Thatcherism had "a project" whose aim was "to transform the political landscape irrevocably: to make us think and speak its language as if there were no other," New Labour is rather "a series of pragmatic adjustments and adaptive moves to essentially Thatcherite terrain."[15] In other words, Thatcherism was a change on the ground of the political; New Labour, despite its claim to "the vision thing," is merely politics.

Although Hall's interventions address politics directly, in the sense of being concerned with electoral politics, tactics, and strategy, his view of the political reflects a broader use of "politics," taking on board, for example, Foucault's notion of power relations as productive and not merely repressive. It can be read as a call to repoliticization, together with an acknowledgment that this is not a once-and-for-all thing but a continuous process. His criticism of the left in Britain is that it has refused this challenge, staying instead *within* the framework, *within* the limits, of the social order established by Thatcherism.

There is, as we have seen, a close connection between subjectivity and ideology. A political project produces "political subjects" through processes of ideological contestation and struggle: It does not rearrange pre-existing subjects. This is so in the case of black identities, too, and Hall addresses the political issues that "the end of the essential black subject" entails. We saw in the discussion of feminism in Chapter 4 that the fiction of essentialism can be politically useful at times. Indeed Derrida argues for a double process in the contestation of any dichotomies such as male/female or white/black, a process of reversal and one of displacement. It may at times be necessary to remain with the reversal, even if only to retain some purchase, some means of critique. But in the loss of the essentialist black subject, Hall sees not the threat of "the collapse of an entire political world" but something else: "extraordinary relief at the passing away of what at one time seemed to be a necessary fiction: . . . either that all black people are good or indeed that all black people are the *same*."[16] This is accompanied by an appreciation of the complexities and ambiguities inherent in the process of subjectivity or identification, where, as we have seen in discussions of Lacan, desire and the gaze are implicated. At this point questions of racism are crossed irrevocably with questions of sexuality,[17] and the specificity of the diasporic experience becomes significant. It is what Hall calls "the politics of living identity through difference":

> the politics of recognising that all of us are composed of multiple social identities, not of one. That we are all complexly constructed through different categories, of different antagonisms, and these may have the effect of locating us socially in multiple positions of marginality and subordination, but which do not yet operate on us in exactly the same way. . . . Any counter politics . . . which attempts to organize people through their diversity of identifications has to be a struggle which is conducted positionally.[18]

This is the Gramscian notion of a "war of position," a struggle in which there are no guarantees of success because identifications are continuously shifting and can be articulated in numerous ways. It means a politics of the contingent, the temporary articulation of differences, and not their overcoming or disappearance. It cannot call up the past as a guarantee either, although the past limits what can be done. But the return to the past "is never a return of a direct or literal kind. The past is not waiting for us back there to recoup our identities against. It is always retold, rediscovered, reinvented. It has to be narrativised. We go to our own pasts through history, through memory, through desire, not as a literal fact."[19]

The role of time and the past is central as well to Homi Bhabha's reading of Frantz Fanon's "The Fact of Blackness."[20] According to Bhabha, Fanon's argument is not just about the historicity of the black man but about "the temporality of modernity within which the figure of the 'human' comes to be authorised." What is important here is Fanon's notion of what Bhabha calls "the belatedness of the black man."[21] The ontology of the white world is based on forms of rationality and notions of progress that rely on linear notions of time. Although Fanon disrupts these, this does "not simply make the question of ontology inappropriate for black identity, but somehow impossible for the very understanding of humanity in the world of modernity."[22] Through a performance of what it means to be not only black but displaced, diasporic, and marginalized, Fanon does not just reverse the hierarchy black/white; he reveals the historicity of the symbol of the universal subject, Man, upon which that metaphysics is based. He reveals how universalism is founded upon the very notion of white supremacy:

> From the perspective of a postcolonial "belatedness," Fanon disturbs the *punctum* of man as the signifying, subjectifying category of Western culture, as a unifying reference of ethical value. Fanon performs the desire of the colonized to identify with the humanistic, enlightenment ideal of Man: "all I wanted was to be a man among other men. I wanted to come lithe and young into a world that was ours and build it together." Then, in

a catachrestic reversal he shows how, despite the pedagogies of human history, the performative discourse of the liberal West, its quotidian conversation and comments, reveal the cultural supremacy and racial typology upon which the universalism of Man is founded. "But of course, come in, sir, there is no colour prejudice among us. . . . Quite, the Negro is a man like ourselves. . . . It is not because he is black that he is less intelligent than we are."23

This provides in one sense a fourth decentering of the subject, to add to those discussed in Chapter 2. Postcolonial critique challenges the historical constructions of modernity. The claim is that "racism" is not just a holdover from earlier periods or from archaic conceptions of the subject but an integral part of modernity's humanistic traditions. The time-lagged colonial and postcolonial moment is written out or forgotten in an attempt to "normalize" it, and this must be resisted.24 What is dismissed as merely the past or history is rather to be seen as what we have called the "constitutive outside" of modernity. Or as Bhabha puts it, speaking in terms of the Lacanian notion of excess or surplus, "What is in modernity *more* than modernity is the disjunctive 'postcolonial' time and space that makes its presence felt *at the level of enunciation*."25 Postcolonial critique is aimed "at transforming the conditions of enunciation at the level of the sign— where the intersubjective realm is constituted—not simply setting up new symbols of identity, new 'positive images' that fuel an unreflective 'identity politics.'"26 In other words, it aims to engage with "the political."

DISCOURSE, IDENTITY, AND ANTAGONISM

In something of a contrast to Hall's work, Laclau and Mouffe's book is an explicit attempt to use insights from the work on discourse of so-called poststructuralist theorists, particularly Foucault, Derrida, and Lacan, to replace the Marxist account of ideology and the social. Laclau claims that there are two approaches to ideology within the Marxist tradition: ideology as a level of the social totality and ideology as false consciousness. Each, he says, is "grounded in an essentialist conception of both society and social agency."27 "Postmodernism" rejects this. Against an essentialist version of a "social totality," Laclau poses the contemporary ("postmodern") view of the "infinitude of the social": "If we maintain the relational character of any identity and if, at the same time, we renounce the *fixation* of those identities into a system [an essence], then the social must be identified with the infinite play of differences, that is, with what in the strictest sense of the term we can call *discourse*."28 The second movement is to examine the attempt to produce this "impossible fixation," to "hegemonize" it. Such attempts are specific to specific social formations, because each has "its own forms of determination and relative autonomy. . . . With this insight, the base-superstructure distinction falls and, along with it, the conception of ideology as a necessary level of every social formation."[29] We are left with the concept of hegemony as producing a temporary, "impossible" society.

In a similar way, Laclau claims the approach to ideology as false consciousness "only makes sense if the identity of the social agent can be fixed."[30] He concludes that since "the identity and homogeneity of social agents [are] an *illusion*, . . . any social subject is *essentially* decentred" and the theoretical ground that made sense of the concept of false consciousness has "evidently dissolved."[31] Instead of proposing that we abandon the concept of ideology, however, Laclau suggests that we maintain it but with an inversion of its traditional content:

> The ideological would not consist of the misrecognition of a positive essence, but exactly the opposite: it would consist of the non-recognition of the precarious character of any positivity, of the impossibility of any ultimate suture. The ideological would consist of those discursive forms through which a society tries to institute itself as such on the basis of closure, of the fixation of meaning. . . . Insofar as the social is impossible without some fixation of meaning, without the discourse of closure, the ideological must be seen as constitutive of the social. Society only exists as the vain attempt to institute that impossible object: society. Utopia is the essence of any communication and social practice.[32]

Laclau and Mouffe first articulated these arguments in *Hegemony and Socialist Strategy,*[33] written at a time when the proliferation of social movements (feminist, green, antinuclear, nationalist, gay) was leading to a questioning of simple concepts of class struggle and their replacement with a politics of identity. Laclau and Mouffe argue that the concept of hegemony "introduces a logic of the social which is incompatible with" the basic categories of Marxist theory.[34] Their approach operates through "a critique and a deconstruction of the various discursive surfaces of classical Marxism."[35] They describe themselves as situated in a post-Marxist terrain, where "it is no longer possible to maintain the conception of subjectivity and classes elaborated by Marxism, nor its vision of the historical course of capitalist development."[36]

Laclau and Mouffe's position is based on a view of a "discursive structure" as "an articulatory practice which constitutes and organises social relations."[37] They construct their notion of articulation by taking concepts from Althusser and radicalizing them—removing what they claim are their essentialist elements. Among these is the concept of "overdetermination."[38] Originally, as Althusser acknowledges, this concept came from psychoanalysis and linguistics.[39] Laclau and Mouffe see "overdetermination" in

Freud as "a very precise type of fusion entailing a symbolic dimension and a plurality of meanings. The concept of overdetermination is constituted in the field of the symbolic."[40] They thus extrapolate Althusser's statement that everything existing in the social is overdetermined to the assertion that "the social constitutes itself as a *symbolic order*."[41] They claim that the logic of overdetermination is

> the incomplete, open and politically negotiable character of every iden-
> tity. . . . Objects appear articulated not like pieces in a clockwork mech-
> anism, but because the presence of some in the others hinders the sutur-
> ing of the identity of any of them. . . . We are in the field of the
> overdetermination of some entities by others, and the relegation of any
> form of paradigmatic fixity to the ultimate horizon of theory.[42]

In this formulation Laclau and Mouffe are incorporating notions from Derridean deconstruction; they are also using the (Lacanian) notion of the social as a symbolic order.

Laclau and Mouffe argue that identity is never fixed, and no discursive formation can emerge as a totality. Only within a *closed* system would it be possible to fix the identity, or "meaning," of each element by its relation with others. In Saussure's analysis of language as a system of differences, the meanings of terms are seen as purely relational, as values. Laclau and Mouffe argue that the idea of a closed system dominated when structuralism was taken from linguistics into the other human sciences: The search became one for underlying structures. The critique of structuralism, poststructuralism, broke with this view of a "fully constituted structural space" but also *retained* the Saussurean move away from language as naming. It did not return to a position where identities are seen as given by relation to a preexisting object: "The resulting conception was of a relational space unable to constitute itself as such—of a field dominated by the *desire* for a structure that was always finally absent. The sign is the name of a split, of an impossible suture between signified and signifier."[43]

As there is no identity that can be fully constituted, "'*society*' is not a valid object of discourse."[44] There is no such thing as society, if by society we mean a fully fixed and defined totality. There is an irresolvable tension between interiority and exteriority at the heart of any social practice. There is no "transcendental signified," in Derrida's terms,[45] but this impossibility of ultimate fixity means there have to be partial fixities. "Any discourse is constituted as an attempt to dominate the field of discursivity, to arrest the flow of differences, to construct a centre."[46] Laclau and Mouffe use the terms "nodal points" (reflecting Lacan's *points de capiton;* see Chapter 5) to describe these "privileged discursive points." For Laclau and Mouffe, "the practice of articulation . . . consists in the construction of nodal points which partially fix meaning; and the partial character of this fixation proceeds from the openness of the social, a result, in its turn, of the constant overflowing of every discourse by the infinitude of the field of discursivity."[47]

The concept of antagonism is central to Laclau and Mouffe's approach and is linked to this lack of closure: "Antagonism, as a witness of the impossibility of a final suture, is the 'experience' of the limit of the social. . . . Antagonisms . . . constitute the limits of society."[48] Antagonism for Laclau and Mouffe is not a contradiction between preexisting concepts nor an opposition between preexisting subjects or identities. It arises in the process of constitution of identities as the limit that makes full constitution as a totality, as a fixed identity, impossible. It is "a relation where in the limits of every objectivity is *shown*" in Wittgenstein's sense. It cannot be *said*, "for every language and every society are constituted as a repression of the consciousness of the impossibility that penetrates them. Antagonism escapes the possibility of being apprehended through language, since language only exists as an attempt to fix that which antagonism subverts."[49] It is important to note here that the notion of "limit" does not refer to a frontier or a boundary as between inside and outside: The limit of the social is *within the social itself*—there is no beyond.

This notion of antagonism is incorporated into a theory of how discursive formations operate politically, through the processes of articulation, hegemony, and the construction of political frontiers. Identity implicates power. Laclau shows, by considering levels of the radicalization of the notion of hegemony, that social relations are always power relations. The first level of radicalization involves the recognition that "floating signifiers" are articulated by the process of hegemonic struggle into different chains or "contents." This version, Laclau claims, still gives too much emphasis to the intentions of social agents and the coherence of their projects. By the time we reach the final level of radicalization, we have moved to a concept of hegemonic articulation as "undecidable in terms of its very formal structure. . . . The hegemonic act will not be the realisation of a rationality preceding it, but an act of radical construction."[50] This links with Derrida's notion of the "undecidable." The implication of this third level is that possibilities that are not "constituted" are repressed; in other words, this is the power relationship. Laclau's thesis is that

> the constitution of a social identity is an act of power and that identity as such is power. . . . Asserting the constitutive nature of antagonism entails asserting the contingent nature of all objectivity and this in turn means that any objectivity is a threatened objectivity. If . . . an objectivity manages to partially affirm itself, it is only by repressing that which threatens it. To study the conditions of existence of a given social identity, then, is

> to study the power mechanisms making it possible. . . . [But] without
> power, there would be no objectivity at all. An objective identity is not a
> homogeneous point but an articulated set of elements.[51]

This view of power and the social leads to a particular view of emancipation: "If power is a prerequisite of any identity, the radical disappearance of power would amount to the disintegration of the social fabric. . . . It is this profound contradiction which underlies any project of *global* emancipation. . . . A harmonious society is impossible because power is the condition for society to be possible (and, at the same time, impossible . . .)."[52] It also has implications for the category of the "subject." Laclau and Mouffe affirm the discursive character of all subject-positions. Some of the debates this leads to are clarified by two examples, the question of the "human being" and the question of the category of "woman." They argue that by seeing both as discursively constructed and nonessentialist, we are then enabled to see the precarious and vulnerable nature of "human," for example, and to struggle more effectively to articulate it to specific other subject-positions. We can also examine the overdetermined nature of the subject-positions involved and the relations between them. Something similar occurs with the category "woman." Lauclau and Mouffe stress the importance of struggle but also the need to recognize that

> overdetermination among the diverse sexual differences produces a systematic effect of sexual division. Every construction of sexual differences . . . invariably constructs the feminine as a pole subordinate to the masculine. . . . The ensemble of social practices, of institutions and discourses which produce woman as a category, are not completely isolated but mutually reinforce and act upon one another. . . . [This is] not the expression of an immutable female essence [but its construction].[53]

In summary, then, Laclau and Mouffe's work leads to an account of the political operation of discursive formations through articulation, hegemony, and the construction of political frontiers that attempts to incorporate Derrida's notion of the undecidable. They argue that ideology should be regarded as the *non*recognition of the impossibility of "society," that is, a closed system, or any essence rather than (as in previous approaches) a *mis*recognition of an essence. They stress the open character and political negotiability of identity and claim that there is no such thing as society—society is impossible. Only partial fixity is possible, through a succession of attempts at hegemony. The notion of antagonism, central to their work, arises as the experience of the *limit* of the social, but this limit is *within* the social, not beyond it: There is no beyond, no extradiscursive realm.

Laclau and Mouffe's approach both depends on and renounces a clear distinction between the "social" and the "political."[54] The political is the moment of antagonism at which power relations are decisive in the constitution of particular social relations as opposed to others that are repressed; the social involves "forgetting" this moment, hence a certain opacity is constitutive of social relations: "If the social is established through the *sedimentation* of the political, through the 'forgetting of origins,' the *reactivation* of the original meaning of the social consists in showing its political essence."[55] In Marx the political is "superstructure," "merely a 'supplement' of the social."[56] For Laclau and Mouffe, the specificity of the political needs to be recognized and theorized. This distinction between "social" and "political" seems to me to be based on a particular view of the social as an arena of consensus and agreed values and the political as one of contestation and struggle. Within this view the concept of ideology is retained, but with a far more limited remit. Ideology is "a discourse which attempts to constitute the social as closed, to construct meanings, and to mute the effects of the infinite play of differences. . . . [Ideology] is a specific will to totality, rather than . . . a belief system of a particular class, or . . . a false consciousness."[57]

Laclau believes that in sociological theory and Marxism, the political has been subordinate to the social, seen as either an "infrastructure" or a branch or a supplement of the social. He argues that we need to invert this relationship:[58] "The central point of . . . postmarxism," he writes, "consists . . . in opposing the 'objectivity' of any kind of ultimate suturing or closure, due to the negativity inherent in the 'constitutive outside.' . . . Accordingly there is a displacement in the very type of valid interrogation."[59] Previously, the particular was seen as an expression of the universal (as Žižek puts it, "law" was incarnated in Roman law and Greek law), whereas in post-Marxism categories such as law are themselves historical and contingent.[60] The problem here is that inverting the relationship between the political and the social still maintains the distinction.

A second and related point is the somewhat contradictory notion of "power" and "society" that Laclau and Mouffe use. The notion of power as constitutive as well as repressive clearly echoes Foucault's concept, discussed in Chapter 3. But power itself, it seems to me, is not sufficiently radicalized in their work. For Laclau and Mouffe, identity is power; but although identity is problematized, power is not. In some sense power is always present, as a prerequisite and as an agent or mechanism. In much the same way, although they regard "society" as impossible and thoroughly question the concept of a harmonious totality, the notion of the social as an entity persists in several parts of their work. They assert, for example, that "the social constitutes itself."[61] The difficulty arises, I would argue, from a tendency to conflate discussions of the constitution of persons as subjects and the constitution of a social collectivity.

This links to the final point of criticism, made by Žižek, which relates to the undertheorization of the subject in *Hegemony and Socialist Strategy*.[62] Laclau and Mouffe's notion of the subject is what Žižek calls a poststructuralist concept of a series of subject-positions, or identities, which are seen as increasingly "fragmenting" to produce a "proliferation" of subjectivities.[63] Although Laclau and Mouffe deny the substantial, pregiven subject, they still have a notion of a series of subject-positions. Granted, these are continually changing as they are rearticulated in differing relations with each other; nevertheless, they are positions into which subjects are, in Althusserian fashion, interpellated. In Laclau and Mouffe's view, subject-positions are constituted as distinct and antagonistic in relation to each other—each is prevented from becoming fully identical with itself (from constituting itself as fixed or essential) through its difference from the other. This produces the illusion that it is the external enemy that prevents the complete achievement of full identity.

Žižek argues that "every identity is already blocked, marked by an impossibility, and the external enemy is simply the small piece, the rest of reality upon which we 'project' or 'externalise' this intrinsic, immanent impossibility."[64] This leads to a radically different view from that of Laclau and Mouffe in relation to the repressive nature of power and the possibility of emancipation. For Žižek,

> There is a certain fundamental, radical, constitutive, self-inflicted impediment, a hindrance of the drive, and the role of the fascinating figure of external Authority, of its repressive force, is to make us blind to this self-impediment of the drive. That is why we could say that it is precisely in the moment when we achieve victory over the enemy in the antagonistic struggle in social reality that we experience the antagonism in its most radical dimension, as a self-hindrance: far from enabling us finally to achieve full identity with ourselves, the moment of victory is the moment of greatest loss . . . "the loss of the loss": the experience that we never had what we were supposed to have lost.[65]

"POLITICS" AS METAPHOR FOR THE ACT

The achievement of Laclau and Mouffe's book, according to Žižek, is its conception of the sociosymbolic field as "structured around a certain impossibility, around a certain fissure which cannot be symbolised."[66] This "social antagonism" is homologous to the Lacanian notion of the "Real," and Laclau and Mouffe's work contributes, as we saw in Chapter 6, to Žižek's development of this conceptualization in his social and ideological analyses.

The political moment, whether the founding moment of a social totality in revolution or a more prosaic moment of an endless process of decisioning, is a moment that produces the "subject" as such, but it is the subject as what Žižek calls the "vanishing mediator."[67] In such a moment, the subject reduces itself "to a mere moment of the totality engendered by its own act."[68] As we saw, in Žižek's analysis the subject and the social or symbolic order are produced in the same moment (one that Lacan called the third "moment" of logical time, the "moment of conclusion"),[69] the moment at which the subject posits the existence of the social order, an act that brings that order into existence. This moment of production of the subject is paradoxical, however. In Žižek's words:

> The moment when the subject "posits his presuppositions" is the very moment of his effacement as subject, *the moment he vanishes as mediator:* the moment of closure when the subject's act of decision changes into its opposite; establishes a new symbolic network by means of which History again acquires the self-evidence of a linear evolution.[70]

This is what Lacan calls an "act" as distinct from action: "a move that . . . defines its own conditions; retroactively produces grounds which justify it."[71] The production of the subject is exactly such an act, in that it (retroactively) produces the social or symbolic order in which the subject finds a place. The act of "self-constitution" as subject, an act that involves presupposing the existence of the symbolic order, is thus seen as the most intensely political act.[72] It is only an act of this form, in contrast to action of a more ordinary, "rule-following," technical, depoliticized kind, that Lacan calls an "act." The act in this sense is also performative "in a way which exceeds the 'speech act': its performativity is 'retroactive': it defines the network of its own presuppositions."[73]

The act in this sense is also by definition illegal: The act violates the laws of the preceding social order. Any "act" as such must by definition do this, as it retroactively defines *its own* conditions. If the act succeeds, that is, if it institutes a "new harmony," a new social or symbolic order, it also loses its criminal character: "An act 'succeeds' the moment it 'sutures' anew its own past, its own conditions, effacing its scandalous character—the act is the emergence of a new master-signifier."[74] The radical contingency of the act as such then disappears, and the act and the new structures or the new "politics" it puts into place seem part of the flow of history. Its success can then and only then be seen as not merely fortuitous or secured by force and violence but as following from the previous course of historical progress. In this way the "act" is similar to the "decision": Both disappear.

What the act does is produce a master signifier that resecures, rescues or resutures, the social order. The new master signifier writes its own history and produces the present as the continuation of the past. It removes the abyss of the decision, erasing the moment of the political, establishing new relations of power and setting in place a new "régime of truth." It provides the certainty that guarantees the subject and responds to its need for reassurance.

As we saw in Chapter 1, this argument can be taken a step further, to provide an account of the role of (what I call) politics. Žižek proposes that "politics" is a metaphor of the political subject, "the element which, within the constituted social space, holds the place of the Political as negativity which suspends it and founds it anew."[75] In other words, "politics" is taking the place of the master signifier as the element that conceals the "lack" in the system, in effect "hiding" the absence of "the political." So, ironically, it is the function of "politics" as subsystem of the social order to conceal the lack in or depoliticization of the social order as such. This concealment is what holds together the social and enables the symbolic order to constitute itself. The "real" of the political is excluded.

In this sense, "politics" as master signifier performs a function similar to that served by the notion of "sovereignty"; the two are perhaps interrelated insofar as the modern nation-state is viewed as an element in the international system. Sovereignty holds the place of the master signifier around which the sovereign state of contemporary political life is founded.[76] The metaphorical significance of "politics" explains why the notion of a *generalized* politics, like Derrida's generalized writing, is such a threat and why it is resisted. Politics as subsystem reflects (and conceals) the way that the social order is a *particular* resolution of the antagonism at the root of the social: "The stable network of 'sub-systems' is the very form of harmony of one pole in the social antagonism, the 'class peace' the very index of the hegemony of one class in the class struggle."[77] Any deconstruction of the notion of politics, any attempt at a repoliticization or a displacement by the notion of a generalized "political," where "everything is political," threatens that order and the relations of power that it embodies.

Such a move is in its nature more of a challenge than a reversal or interchange of the hierarchy of "politics" and "economics" as explanatory factors, for example, might be. The crucial point is that the status of "politics" as metaphor or ideological element vanishes once the social order is produced. The subsystem of "politics" loses its distinctiveness and becomes one among a number of subsystems of the social order:

> What is lost once the network of "sub-systems" is stabilised—that is to say, once the "new harmony" is established, once the new Order "posits its presuppositions," "sutures" its field—is the *metaphoricity* of the element which represents its genesis: this element is reduced to being "one among the others"; it loses its character of *One which holds the place of Nothing* (of radical negativity).[78]

If the metaphoricity or ideological status of "politics" as element can be made visible again—or in other words, if what we call the political system can be repoliticized—the stability of the whole system, the existing social order, can be challenged. Otherwise challenges in the name of "politics" do not address the system as such; rather than challenging it, they paradoxically reinforce and re-produce it by reinstalling perpetually the invisibility of the foundational moment. They contribute to its naturalization, technologization, and depoliticization.

Theories of international relations can be complicit in this process of concealment. As R. B. J. Walker has pointed out, they are "expressions of the limits of modern politics [that] reveal some of the crucial conditions under which modern political life is possible at all, as well as the conditions under which alternatives to the present have been rendered implausible or even unthinkable."[79] Theories of international relations contribute to the depoliticization of the international and the domestic every time they take for granted the separation of the two, with the domestic realm within the sovereign state being seen as the realm of "political community" and the international arena as the domain of anarchy, where political or ethical community is replaced by power politics in some raw state of nature.

This separation is for some (but by no means all) scholars the very self-definition of the "discipline," and it claims a past as well as a present; it traces its origins and analyzes its Westphalian genesis. The concept of sovereignty plays a crucial part in delimiting domestic "politics." As with the master signifier "politics," however, that of "sovereignty" erases the traces of its own historicity. In Walker's words again, international relations theory is

> a discourse that systematically reifies an historically specific spatial ontology, a sharp delineation of here and there, a discourse that both expresses and constantly affirms the presence and absence of political life inside and outside the modern state as the only ground on which structural necessities can be understood and new realms of freedom and history can be revealed.[80]

A repoliticization of international relations would involve at the very least *not forgetting* that sovereignty and the situating of politics within the state and anarchy outside is only one possible solution to the problem of political community. Moreover, addressing Hindess's argument (discussed in Chapter 1), it would acknowledge that political community is not the question in any case, that we need instead to find "a way to think about politics in the absence of its defining, constitutive fiction."[81] The notion of "political community" itself implies a distinction from some other community—economic, social, and so forth—in other words, "political community" accepts as given the concept of "politics" as subsystem. It demands that we solve the problem within the confines of the existing social order and rules out "the political" moment. The distinctions it takes for granted are those very distinctions that reflect the *political* settlement within which present relations of power flourish and conceal its political, contingent, and violent nature. The power of "the role of fictional communities in the social and political thinking of western societies"[82] is what should be problematized.

REPOLITICIZATION AND THE INTELLECTUAL

In a sense, the duty of the critical intellectual is exactly this *not forgetting,* this drawing of attention to the "'produced,' artificial, contingent character"[83] of any reigning master signifier. This is arguably the standpoint of any critical theory with a claim to an intellectual response or responsibility. The academic attitude, almost by definition, relies on the notion of an independence or distance from the accepted authority of the age, a notion of questioning what is "given." Foucault points to the distinction between the "specific" intellectual, caught up in "real, material, everyday struggles," and the "universal" intellectual, involved as a spokesperson of the universal, a figure of authority. The specific intellectual is the expert of technoscientific truth, and as such he or she is in a unique position to struggle at the level of the general régime of truth that underpins the social order. There is a battle "for truth"; or in Foucault's words:

> The essential political problem for the intellectual is . . . the political, economic, institutional régime of the production of truth. It's not a matter of emancipating truth from every system of power (which would be a chimera, for truth is already power) but of detaching the power of truth from the forms of hegemony, social, economic and cultural, within which it operates at the present time. The political question . . . is truth itself.[84]

As Derrida's work makes clear, however, it is not easy to detach oneself from the existing phallogocentric régime of truth and retain any critical purchase, which would allow a political act or intervention. From a feminist perspective, Irigaray argues (as we saw in Chapter 2) that "there is no simple manageable way to leap to the outside of phallogocentrism."[85] But she suggests that the power of logocentric "truth" relies as much on being taken seriously as anything else. In other words, it relies on forgetting the joke, forgetting the precariousness of logocentrism's seeming naturalness. Disrupting this claim to seriousness can help; this means "not to forget to laugh. Not to forget that the dimension of desire, of pleasure, is untranslatable, unrepresentable, irrecuperable, in the 'seriousness'—the adequacy, the univocity, the truth . . . —of a discourse that claims to state its meaning."[86] Again the call is not to forget. To return to "the political," we must move away from the realm of *truth* and toward that of *desire.* Or rather, we must move toward a reconsideration of the desire for truth or certainty that conjures up the master signifier in the first place. Is there a possibility of escaping that desire for completion that produces the depoliticization we have seen? What does this mean for the call not to forget?

To enact a repoliticization requires an acceptance of the impossibility of ontological fullness.[87] This ontological paradox appears in theoretical physics, where two complementary properties of a subatomic particle are mutually exclusive—it is only possible to know one or the other to the necessary degree of accuracy. This notion of complementarity is reflected in the way "the subject is forced to choose and accept a certain fundamental loss or impossibility" in a Lacanian act.[88] As Žižek puts it, "My reflective awareness of all the circumstances which condition my act can never lead me to act: it cannot explain the fact of the act itself. By endlessly weighing the reasons for and against, I never manage to act—at a certain point I must decide to 'strike out blindly.'"[89] The act has to take place without justification, without foundation in knowledge, without guarantee or legitimacy. It cannot be grounded in ontology; it is this "crack" that gives rise to ethics: "There is ethics—that is to say, an injunction which cannot be grounded in ontology—in so far as there is a crack in the ontological edifice of the universe: at its most elementary, ethics designates fidelity to this crack."[90]

Žižek argues that the "paradox of complementarity," or what Derrida calls the "logic of the decision," should not be shirked. The lack of ontological fullness leads to a paradox that lies in the way the political act entails, for its very effectivity, some reference to the ethical. What we should avoid is

the illusion of a politics delivered from naturalising mystification, dispensing with any reference to some extra-political foundation . . . as if naturalisation—that is, a reference to some non-antagonistic neutral (ethical) foundation—illusory as it is, were not an irreducible, necessary condition of a politically efficient *prise de position*. In this precise sense, ethics is a *supplement* of the political: there is no political "taking sides" without minimal reference to some ethical normativity which transcends the sphere of the purely Political—in other words: without the minimal "naturalisation" involved in legitimating our position via reference to some extra-political (natural, ethical, theological . . .) agency.[91]

This recalls the discussion in Chapter 4 of Derrida's notion of deconstruction as a double science, a movement both of reversal and displacement. As we saw there, it is necessary at times to retain and make political use of the dichotomy one is trying to challenge, in order for the challenge to have some purchase in discursive practice. This is what Žižek, too, is arguing. The result is a position of accepting that "one cannot simultaneously 'know it' and 'do it,'" which translates into a farewell to "the Enlightenment illusion of a self transparent activity."[92]

It should be noted that the notion of *not forgetting* involved in re-politicization is not equivalent to a historical remembering, the sort of memory that produces a narrative account or attempts to reproduce the appearance of reality in past events. It is instead an encircling of the trauma, the unsymbolizable real: Our duty is "to keep alive the memory of all lost causes, of all shattered and perverted dreams and hopes."[93] Thus Žižek's Lacanian ethics is "an ethics grounded in reference to the traumatic Real which resists symbolisation, the Real which is experienced in the encounter with the abyss of the Other's desire."[94]

The remembering involved is the drive or "the ethical compulsion which compels us to mark repeatedly the memory of a lost Cause."[95] The point is not to record or document or reenact a past trauma, which would "gentrify" and neutralize it. What is crucial about trauma is the impossibility of integrating it into the symbolic order: The Real is precisely that which cannot be symbolized, the surplus that remains. What is needed is "to *encircle* again and again the site of the lost Thing, to *mark* its very impossibility."[96] The most basic form of this marking is a tombstone that marks a burial site. A similar gesture is that of a survivor of Auschwitz who remains living nearby so that he can revisit the site; the only important thing is that he returns, as a mute witness. As Žižek says, "All we have to do is to mark repeatedly the trauma as such, in its very 'impossibility,' in its non-integrated horror, by means of some 'empty' symbolic gesture."[97]

Foucault reminds us that "everything is dangerous. . . . The ethical political choice we have to make every day is to determine which is the main danger."[98] It is not the task of the international relations theorist to secure us (whatever community "we" may be) against the danger but precisely the reverse: to challenge the hegemony of the power relations or symbolic order in whose name security is produced, to render visible its contingent, provisional nature. This leads to a position that advocates a continual political involvement and a need for recurring, vigilant, and responsive activism. We should repeatedly mark the trauma and ensure that we are not lulled into forgetfulness.

NOTES

1. Slavoj Žižek, *For They Know Not What They Do: Enjoyment as a Political Factor* (London: Verso, 1991), 193.

2. Jacques Derrida, "'Eating Well,' or the Calculation of the Subject: An Interview with Jacques Derrida," in *Who Comes After the Subject?* ed. Eduardo Cadava, Peter Connor, and Jean-Luc Nancy (New York: Routledge, 1991), 108.

3. For a recent overview of Hall's work and some critical commentary, see the discussions in David Morley and Kuan-Hsing Chen, eds., *Stuart Hall: Critical Dialogues in Cultural Studies* (London: Routledge, 1996).

4. Lawrence Grossberg, "On Postmodernism and Articulation: An Interview with Stuart Hall," reprinted in ibid., 149.

5. His works include Stuart Hall, "The Hinterland of Science: Ideology and the 'Sociology of Knowledge,'" in *On Ideology,* ed. Bill Schwartz (London: Hutchinson, for the Centre for Contemporary Cultural Studies, University of Birmingham, 1977), 9–32; Stuart Hall, Bob Lumley, and Gregor McLennan, "Politics and Ideology: Gramsci," in Schwartz, *On Ideology,* 45–76; "Recent Developments in Theories of Language and Ideology: A Critical Note," in *Culture, Media, Language: Working Papers in Cultural Studies, 1972–1979,* ed. Stuart Hall (London: Routledge, in association with the Centre for Contemporary Cultural Studies, University of Birmingham, 1980), 157–162; Stuart Hall, "The Rediscovery of 'Ideology': Return of the Repressed in Media Studies," in *Culture, Society and the Media,* ed. Michael Gurevitch et al. (London: Methuen, 1982), 56–90; and "Religious Ideologies and Social Movements in Jamaica," in *Religion and Ideology,* ed. Robert Bocock and Kenneth Thompson (Manchester, UK: Manchester University Press, 1985), 269–296. On postcolonialism, nationalism, and cultural studies, see for example, Stuart Hall, "Culture, Community, Nation," *Cultural Studies,* 7, 3 (1993): 349–363.

6. Grossberg, "On Postmodernism and Articulation," 142.

7. Ernesto Laclau, *Politics and Ideology in Marxist Theory* (Oxford: Blackwell, 1979).

8. V. N. Vološinov, *Marxism and the Philosophy of Language,* trans. Ladislav Matejka and I. R. Titunik (Cambridge: Harvard University Press, 1986). The relationship of this book to Mikhail Bakhtin's work is discussed in the translator's preface.

9. Stuart Hall, "For Allon White: Metaphors of Transformation," in Morley and Chen, *Stuart Hall,* 297.

10. Stuart Hall, "The Great Moving Right Show," reprinted in *The Hard Road to Renewal: Thatcherism and the Crisis of the Left* (London: Verso, 1988), 39–56; Stuart Hall, "The Great Moving Nowhere Show," *Marxism Today,* November/December 1998, 9–14.

11. Stuart Hall, Chas Critcher, Tony Jefferson, John Clarke, and Brian Roberts, *Policing the Crisis: Mugging, the State, and Law and Order* (London: Macmillan, 1978).

12. Hall, *Hard Road to Renewal,* 7.

13. Ibid.

14. Ibid., 6.

15. Hall, "The Great Moving Nowhere Show," 9.

16. Stuart Hall, "New Ethnicities," in Morley and Chen, *Stuart Hall,* 444.

17. Ibid., 445. The work of Frantz Fanon is central here, particularly *Black Skin, White Masks* (London: Pluto, 1991).

18. Stuart Hall, "Old and New Identities, Old and New Ethnicities," in *Culture, Globalisation and the World System,* ed. Anthony D. King (Basingstoke, UK: Macmillan Education, 1991), 57.

19. Ibid., 58.

20. Fanon's "The Fact of Blackness," in *Black Skin, White Masks.*

21. Homi Bhabha, *The Location of Culture* (London: Routledge, 1994), 236.

22. Ibid., 236–237.

23. Ibid., 237.

24. Ibid., 251.

25. Ibid.

26. Ibid., 247.

27. Ernesto Laclau, "The Impossibility of Society," in *New Reflections on the Revolution of Our Time,* ed. Ernesto Laclau (London: Verso, 1990), 89.

28. Ibid., 90.

29. Ibid., 91.

30. Ibid.

31. Ibid., 92 (my emphasis).

32. Ibid. This is sometimes expressed as the claim that ideology as such relates only to totalitarian societies, whereas I have read Laclau as claiming ideology in every (attempt at) social totality. Ssee, for example, David Howarth, "Discourse Theory," in *Theory and Methods in Political Science,* ed. David Marsh and Gerry Stoker (London: Macmillan, 1995), 115–133.

33. Ernesto Laclau and Chantal Mouffe, *Hegemony and Socialist Strategy: Towards a Radical Democratic Politics* (London: Verso, 1985).

34. Ibid., 3.

35. Ibid.

36. Ibid., 4. Laclau and Mouffe attempt to demonstrate that "the space of the economy is itself structured as a political space, and that in it, as in any other 'level' of society, those practices . . . characterised as hegemonic are fully operative" (ibid., 77). They do this in two ways. First, they argue that the Marxist conception of labor power as a commodity is a "fiction"—that, on the contrary, the extraction by capital of the use value (labor) from the labor power it had purchased was much more problematic than was the case for any other commodity in the production process. It involved at its heart a series of relations of domination: Thus the evolution of the labor process cannot occur without struggle. It is not the pure logic of the process of capital accumulation that determines it, but the (political) process of struggle and domination. Second, they argue that we have seen the decentering of the working class as a single coherent subject. There is no working-class subject constituted by a single logic of the economic. "It is impossible to talk today about the homogeneity of the working class, and . . . to trace it to a mechanism inscribed in the logic of capitalist accumulation" (ibid., 82). Hence it is not possible to retain the idea of workers' identity based on common economic interests.

37. Ibid., 96. Laclau and Mouffe define their terms as follows: "We will call *articulation* any practice establishing a relation among elements such that their identity is modified as a result of the articulatory practice. The structured totality resulting from the articulatory practice, we will call *discourse*" (ibid., 105). For the coherence they attribute to a "discursive formation," they turn to Foucault—the Foucault of the *Archaeology of Knowledge.* Dispersion is the principle of unity, but "no discursive formation is a sutured totality" (Laclau and Mouffe, *Hegemony,* 106). They reject the distinction between discursive and nondiscursive practices and stress that their assertion that every object is constituted as an object of discourse "has nothing to do with whether there is a world external to thought, or with the realism/idealism opposition" (ibid., 108). They also stress their view of the material character of discursive structures. They reject the assumption of the mental character of discourse. Ideologies are not simple systems of ideas but are "embodied in institutions, rituals and so forth" (ibid., 109).

38. See Louis Althusser, "Contradiction and Overdetermination," in *For Marx* (London: Allen Lane/Penguin, 1969), 87–128.

39. See my discussions of Saussure and Freud in Chapter 2.

40. Laclau and Mouffe, *Hegemony,* 97.

41. Ibid., 97–98 (my emphasis).

42. Ibid., 104–105.

43. Ibid., 113 (my emphasis).

44. Ibid., 111.

45. Jacques Derrida, *Writing and Difference,* trans. Alan Bass (London: Routledge, 1978), 280.

46. Laclau and Mouffe, *Hegemony,* 112.

47. Ibid., 113. In their discussion they bring in but do not elaborate on the notion of desire, in the sense of the desire for totality or closure. We saw these concepts, together with the notion of the social as a symbolic order, in Žižek.

48. Ibid., 125.

49. Ibid.

50. Ernesto Laclau, "New Reflections on the Revolutions of Our Time," in Laclau, *New Reflections,* 3–85.

51. Ibid., 31–32.

52. Ibid., 33.

53. Laclau and Mouffe, *Hegemony,* 118.

54. In arguing that economic relations are politically constituted, Laclau and Mouffe are reversing the Marxist base-superstructure relationship. Despite this, it could be argued that Laclau still has a very rationalistic-objectivist view of the political strongly grounded in Marxist feelings of the importance of reality and the economic. This can be seen, for example, when he argues, "There is something in contemporary capitalism which really tends to multiply dislocations and create new antagonisms" (Laclau, "New Reflections," 41).

55. Ernesto Laclau, "Letter to Aletta," in Laclau, *New Reflections,* 160.

56. Ibid., 161.

57. Aletta Norval, "Letter to Ernesto," in Laclau, *New Reflections,* 135–157.

58. The subsequent history of Marxism is the "revenge of the supplement."

59. Laclau, "Letter to Aletta," 161.

60. Laclau argues that both approaches can be found in Marxism. There are two strands of Marxism: that represented in the "Preface to 'A Critique of Political Economy'" and that represented in the *Manifesto of the Communist Party.* In the "Preface" history proceeds as a result of the development of the productive forces, in the *Manifesto* by the process of class struggle. In the first form of Marxism, we proceed from universals to historical cases, with deviations from the expected course of history viewed as accidents, caused by something radically "exterior" to the process. "Understanding history . . . consists of an operation of recognition in which essential actors, whose fundamental identity is known in advance, are identified with the empirical actors personifying them" (Laclau, "New Reflections," 22). In the second form, we take a historical approach and view all "objects" or social agents as radically contingent: "There is thus a historicisation of the categories of social analysis" (ibid.). Laclau argues that we need to move beyond the essentialist basis of both these approaches.

61. Laclau and Mouffe, *Hegemony,* 97–98.

62. Slavoj Žižek, "Beyond Discourse Analysis," in Laclau, *New Reflections,* 249–260.

63. There are elements of this view in Hall's work, too.

64. Žižek, "Beyond Discourse Analysis," 252.

65. Ibid.

66. Ibid., 249.

67. Žižek, *For They Know Not What They Do,* 190–191.

68. Ibid., 191.

69. Slavoj Žižek, *The Indivisible Remainder: An Essay on Schelling and Related Matters* (London: Verso, 1996), 135.

70. Žižek, *For They Know Not What They Do,* 190.

71. Ibid., 192.

72. This gives a new slant to the slogan "the personal is political" or, in Cynthia Enloe's version, "the personal is international." Cynthia Enloe, *Bananas, Beaches and Bases: Making Feminist Sense of International Politics* (Berkeley: University of California Press, 1990).

73. Žižek, *For They Know Not What They Do,* 192.

74. Ibid., 192–193.

75. Ibid., 194.

76. Jenny Edkins and Véronique Pin-Fat, "The Subject of the Political," in *Sovereignty and Subjectivity,* ed. Jenny Edkins, Nalini Persram, and Véronique Pin-Fat (Boulder, CO: Lynne Rienner, 1999), 1–18.

77. Žižek, *For They Know Not What They Do,* 195.

78. Ibid.

79. R. B. J. Walker, *Inside/Outside: International Relations as Political Theory* (Cambridge: Cambridge University Press, 1993), x.

80. Ibid., ix.

81. Barry Hindess, *Discourses of Power: From Hobbes to Foucault* (Oxford: Blackwell, 1996), 158.

82. Ibid.

83. Slavoj Žižek, *Tarrying with the Negative: Kant, Hegel and the Critique of Ideology* (Durham, NC: Duke University Press, 1993), 2.

84. Michel Foucault, "Truth and Power," in *Power/Knowledge: Selected Interviews and Other Writings, 1972–1977,* ed. Colin Gordon (Brighton, UK: Harvester, 1980), 133.

85. Luce Irigaray, *This Sex Which Is Not One,* trans. Catherine Porter with Carolyn Burke (Ithaca, NY: Cornell University Press, 1985), 162.

86. Ibid., 163.

87. For a discussion of the notion of "ontological fullness," see Edkins and Pin-Fat, "The Subject of the Political."

88. Žižek, *Indivisible Remainder,* 211. This is similar to Derrida's double contradictory imperative, as discussed in Chapter 4.

89. Ibid., 212.

90. Slavoj Žižek, *The Plague of Fantasies* (London: Verso, 1997), 213–214.

91. Žižek, *Indivisible Remainder,* 213.

92. Ibid.

93. Žižek, *For They Know Not What They Do,* 271.

94. Žižek, *Plague of Fantasies,* 213–214.

95. Žižek, *For They Know Not What They Do,* 272.

96. Ibid.

97. Ibid. Žižek sees this as part of the way psychoanalysis can "delimit the space of possible resistance to capital" (ibid., 271) and by maintaining a distance from the present "discern signs of the New" (ibid., 273).

98. Michel Foucault, "On the Genealogy of Ethics: An Overview of Work in Progress," in *The Foucault Reader: An Introduction to Foucault's Thought,* ed. Paul Rabinow (Harmondsworth, UK: Penguin, 1991), 343.

Selected Bibliography

Althusser, Louis. "Contradiction and Overdetermination." In *For Marx*. London: Allen Lane/Penguin Press, 1969, 87–128.

———. "Ideology and Ideological State Apparatuses (Notes Towards an Investigation)," in *Essays on Ideology*. London: Verso, 1984.

Anderson, Mary B. *Do No Harm: How Aid Can Support Peace—or War*. Boulder, CO: Lynne Rienner, 1999.

Ashley, Richard. "The Achievements of Post-Structuralism." In *International Theory: Posivitism and Beyond,* ed. Steve Smith, Ken Booth, and Marysia Zalewski. Cambridge: Cambridge University Press, 1996, 240–253.

Badiou, Alain. *L'Être et l'événement*. Paris: Le Seuil, 1988.

———. *Peut-on penser la politique?* Paris: Le Seuil, 1985.

Barrett, Michèle. *The Politics of Truth: From Marx to Foucault*. Cambridge: Polity, 1991.

Barthes, Roland. *Mythologies*. Trans. Annette Lavers. London: Jonathan Cape, 1972.

Benvenuto, Bice, and Roger Kennedy. *The Works of Jacques Lacan: An Introduction*. London: Free Association Books, 1986.

Bhabha, Homi. *The Location of Culture*. London: Routledge, 1994.

Bowie, Malcolm. *Lacan*. London: Fontana, 1991.

Burchell, Graham, Colin Gordon, and Peter Miller, eds. *The Foucault Effect: Studies in Governmentality with Two Lectures by and an Interview with Michel Foucault*. London: Harvester Wheatsheaf, 1991.

Butler, Judith. *Bodies That Matter: On the Discursive Limits of 'Sex'*. London: Routledge, 1993.

Buzan, Barry, Ole Waever, and Jaap de Wilde. *Security: A New Framework for Analysis*. Boulder, CO: Lynne Rienner, 1998.

Coward, Rosalind, and John Ellis. *Language and Materialism: Developments in Semiology and the Theory of the Subject*. London: Routledge & Kegan Paul, 1977.

Critchley, Simon. *The Ethics of Deconstruction: Derrida and Levinas*. Oxford: Blackwell, 1992.

Culler, Jonathan. *On Deconstruction: Theory and Criticism After Structuralism*. London: Routledge, 1983.

Dallmayr, Fred. *The Other Heidegger*. Ithaca, NY: Cornell University Press, 1993.

Deleuze, Gilles. *Foucault.* Trans. Seán Hand. London: Athlone Press, 1988.

Der Derian, James, and Michael J. Shapiro. *International/Intertextual Relations.* New York: Lexington Books, 1989.

Derrida, Jacques. "The Conflict of Faculties." In *Languages of Knowledge and of Inquiry,* ed. Michael Riffaterre. New York: Columbia University Press, 1982.

———. "'Eating Well,' or the Calculation of the Subject: An Interview with Jacques Derrida." In *Who Comes After the Subject?* ed. Eduardo Cadava, Peter Connor, and Jean-Luc Nancy. New York: Routledge, 1991, 96–119.

———. "Force of Law: The 'Mystical Foundation of Authority.'" In *Deconstruction and the Possibility of Justice,* ed. David Gray Carlson, Drucilla Cornell, and Michel Rosenfeld. Trans. Mary Quaintance. New York: Routledge, 1992, 3–67.

———, ed. *Limited Inc.* Trans. Samuel Weber and Jeffrey Mehlman. Evanston, IL: Northwestern University Press, 1988.

———. *Margins of Philosophy.* Trans. Alan Bass. Chicago: University of Chicago Press, 1982.

———. *Of Grammatology.* Trans. Gayatri Chakravorty Spivak. Baltimore, MD: Johns Hopkins University Press, 1976.

———. *The Other Heading: Reflections on Today's Europe.* Trans. Pascale-Anne Brault and Michael B. Naas. Bloomington: Indiana University Press, 1992.

———. *Positions.* Trans. Alan Bass. London: Athlone Press, 1987.

———. *Writing and Difference.* Trans. Alan Bass. London: Routledge, 1978.

Descartes, René. *Discourse on Method and Other Writings.* Trans. F. E. Sutcliffe. Harmondsworth, UK: Penguin, 1968.

Dews, Peter. "The Tremor of Reflection: Slavoj Zizek's Lacanian Dialectics." *Radical Philosophy,* 72 (1995): 17–29.

Dillon, Michael. *Politics of Security: Towards a Political Philosophy of Continental Thought.* London: Routledge, 1996.

Donald, James, and Stuart Hall. *Politics and Ideology.* Milton Keynes, UK: Open University Press, 1986.

Dor, Joël. *Introduction to the Reading of Lacan: The Unconscious Structured Like a Language,* ed. Judith Feher Gurewich. Trans. Susan Fairfield. Northvale, NJ: Jason Aronson, 1997.

Dreyfus, Hubert L., and Paul Rabinow. *Michel Foucault: Beyond Structuralism and Hermeneutics, with an Afterword by Michel Foucault.* Hemel Hempstead, UK: Harvester, 1994.

Duffield, Mark. "NGOs, Disaster Relief and Asset Transfer in the Horn: Political Survival in a Permanent Emergency." *Development and Change,* 24, 1 (1993): 131–157.

Eagleton, Terry. *Literary Theory: An Introduction.* Oxford: Blackwell, 1983.

Edkins, Jenny. *Famines and Modernity: Pictures of Hunger, Concepts of Famine, Practices of Aid.* Minneapolis: University of Minnesota Press, forthcoming.

———. "International Security." In *Post-Structuralism and Politics: An Introduction,* ed. Alan Finlayson and Jeremy Valentine. Edinburgh: Edinburgh University Press, forthcoming.

———. "Legality with a Vengeance: Famines and Humanitarian Relief in 'Complex Emergencies.'" *Millennium,* 25, 3 (1996): 547–575.

———, ed. "The Politics of Emergency." *Manchester Papers in Politics,* 2, 1997.

Edkins, Jenny, and Véronique Pin-Fat. "The Subject of the Political." In *Sovereignty and Subjectivity,* ed. Jenny Edkins, Nalini Persram, and Véronique Pin-Fat. Boulder, CO: Lynne Rienner, 1999, 1–18.

Elam, Diane. *Feminism and Deconstruction: Ms. en Abyme.* London: Routledge, 1994.

Elshtain, Jean Bethke. *Public Man, Private Woman: Women in Social and Political Thought.* 2nd ed. Princeton, NJ: Princeton University Press, 1993.

Enloe, Cynthia. *Bananas, Beaches and Bases: Making Feminist Sense of International Politics.* Berkeley: University of California Press, 1990.

Ewald, François. Presentation at the Foucault Anniversary Conference, organized by Signs of the Times, London, 25 June 1994.

Fanon, Frantz. *Black Skin White Masks.* London: Pluto, 1991.

Feder, Ellen K., Mary C. Rawlinson, and Emily Zakin, eds. *Derrida and Feminism: Recasting the Question of Woman.* London: Routledge, 1997.

Felman, Shoshana. "Rereading Femininity." *Yale French Studies,* 62 (1981): 42.

Fink, Bruce. *The Lacanian Subject: Between Language and Jouissance.* Princeton, NJ: Princeton University Press, 1995.

Foucault, Michel. *The Archaeology of Knowledge.* Trans. A. M. Sheridan Smith. London: Routledge, 1989.

———. *The Birth of the Clinic: An Archaeology of Medical Perception.* Trans. A. M. Sheridan. London: Tavistock, 1973.

———. *Discipline and Punish: The Birth of the Prison.* Trans. Alan Sheridan. Harmondsworth, UK: Penguin, 1991.

———. *The History of Sexuality,* vol. 1: *An Introduction.* Trans. Robert Hurley. Harmondsworth, UK: Penguin, 1990.

———. *The History of Sexuality,* vol. 2: *The Use of Pleasure.* Trans. Robert Hurley. Harmondsworth, UK: Penguin, 1992.

———. *The History of Sexuality,* vol. 3: *The Care of the Self.* Trans. Robert Hurley. Harmondsworth, UK: Penguin, 1990.

———. *Language, Counter-memory, Practice: Selected Essays and Interviews,* ed. Donald F. Bouchard. Trans. Donald F. Bouchard and Sherry Simon. Ithaca, NY: Cornell University Press, 1977.

———. *Madness and Civilisation: A History of Insanity in the Age of Reason.* Trans. Richard Howard. London: Routledge, 1989.

———. "On the Genealogy of Ethics: An Overview of Work in Progress." In *The Foucault Reader: An Introduction to Foucault's Thought,* ed. Paul Rabinow. Harmondsworth, UK: Penguin, 1991, 340–372.

———. "The Order of Discourse." In *Language and Politics,* ed. Michael J. Shapiro. Trans. Ian McLeod. Oxford: Blackwell, 1984, 108–138.

———. *The Order of Things: An Archaeology of the Human Sciences.* London: Routledge, 1989.

———. *Power/Knowledge: Selected Interviews and Other Writings 1972–1977,* ed. Colin Gordon. Brighton, UK: Harvester, 1980.

———. "The Subject and Power." In *Michel Foucault: Beyond Structuralism and Hermeneutics,* ed. Hubert L. Dreyfus and Paul Rabinow. Hemel Hempstead: Harvester, 1982.

———. "Technologies of the Self." In *Technologies of the Self,* ed. Luther H. Martin, Huck Gutman, and Patrick H. Hutton. Amherst: University of Massachusetts Press, 1988, 16–49.

Fraser, Nancy. "The French Derrideans: Politicising Deconstruction or Deconstructing the Political?" *New German Critique,* 33 (1984): 127–154.

Freud, Sigmund. *The Complete Introductory Lectures on Psychoanalysis.* Trans. James Strachey. London: George Allen and Unwin, 1971.

———. "The Ego and the Id." In *On Metapsychology: The Theory of Psycho-analysis,* ed. Angela Richards. Trans. James Strachey. Harmondsworth, UK: Penguin, 1984.

———. *The Interpretation of Dreams.* Trans. James Strachey. Harmondsworth, UK: Penguin, 1991.

Gadet, Françoise. *Saussure and Contemporary Culture.* Trans. Gregory Elliot. London: Hutchinson Radius, 1989.

Gann, Rose. "The Limits of Textbook Ideology." *Politics,* 15, 2 (1995): 127–133.

Gasché, Rodolphe. *The Tain of the Mirror: Derrida and the Philosophy of Reflection.* Cambridge: Harvard University Press, 1986.

Gerth, H. H., and C. Wright Mills, eds. and trans. *From Max Weber: Essays in Sociology.* London: Routledge, 1948.

Gramsci, Antonio. *Selections from Prison Notebooks.* Ed. and trans. Quintin Hoare and Geoffrey Nowell Smith. London: Lawrence and Wishart, 1971.

Grossberg, Lawrence. "On Postmodernism and Articulation: An Interview with Stuart Hall." In *Stuart Hall: Critical Dialogues in Cultural Studies,* ed. David Morley and Kuan-Hsing Chen. London: Routledge, 1996, 131–150.

Grosz, Elizabeth. *Jacques Lacan: A Feminist Introduction.* London: Routledge, 1990.

———. *Sexual Subversions: Three French Feminists.* St. Leonards, Australia: Allen & Unwin, 1989.

Hall, Stuart. "Culture, Community, Nation." *Cultural Studies,* 7, 3 (1993): 349–363.

———. "For Allon White: Metaphors of Transformation." In *Stuart Hall: Critical Dialogues in Cultural Studies.* ed. David Morley and Kuan-Hsing Chen. London: Routledge, 1996, 287–305.

———. "The Great Moving Nowhere Show," *Marxism Today,* November/December 1998, 9–14.

———. "The Great Moving Right Show." In *The Hard Road to Renewal: Thatcherism and the Crisis of the Left.* London: Verso, 1988, 39–56.

———. "The Hinterland of Science: Ideology and the 'Sociology of Knowledge.'" In *On Ideology,* ed. Bill Schwartz. London: Hutchinson, for the Centre for Contemporary Cultural Studies, University of Birmingham, 1977, 9–32.

———. "New Ethnicities." In *Stuart Hall: Critical Dialogues in Cultural Studies,* ed. David Morley and Kuan-Hsing Chen. London: Routledge, 1996, 441–449.

———. "Old and New Identities, Old and New Ethnicities." In *Culture, Globalisation and the World System,* ed. Anthony D. King. Basingstoke, UK: Macmillan Education, 1991.

———. "The Question of Cultural Identity." In *Modernity and Its Futures,* ed. Stuart Hall, David Held, and Tony McGrew. London: Polity, in association with the Open University, 1992, 273–325.

———. "Recent Developments in Theories of Language and Ideology: A Critical Note." In *Culture, Media, Language: Working Papers in Cultural Studies, 1972–1979,* ed. Stuart Hall. London: Routledge, in association with the Centre for Contemporary Cultural Studies, University of Birmingham, 1980, 157–162.

———. "The Rediscovery of 'Ideology': Return of the Repressed in Media Studies." In *Culture, Society and the Media,* ed. Michael Gurevitch et al. London: Methuen, 1982, 56–90.

———. "Religious Ideologies and Social Movements in Jamaica." In *Religion and Ideology,* ed. Robert Bocock and Kenneth Thompson. Manchester, UK: Manchester University Press, 1985, 269–296.

Hall, Stuart, Bob Lumley, and Gregor McLennan. "Politics and Ideology: Gramsci." In *On Ideology,* ed. Bill Schwartz. London: Hutchinson, for the Centre for Contemporary Cultural Studies, Birmingham, 1977, 45–76.

Hall, Stuart, Chas Critcher, Tony Jefferson, John Clarke, and Brian Roberts. *Policing the Crisis: Mugging, the State, and Law and Order.* London: Macmillan, 1978.

Hindess, Barry. *Discourses of Power: From Hobbes to Foucault.* Oxford: Blackwell, 1996.

Hollis, Martin, and Steve Smith. *Explaining and Understanding International Relations.* Oxford: Oxford University Press, 1990.

Howarth, David. "Discourse Theory." In *Theory and Methods in Political Science,* ed. David Marsh and Gerry Stoker. London: Macmillan, 1995, 115–133.

Ingram, David. "The Retreat of the Political in the Modern Age: Jean-Luc Nancy on Totalitarianism and Community." *Research on Phenomenology,* 18 (1988): 93–124.

Irigaray, Luce. *Je, Tu, Nous: Toward a Culture of Difference.* Trans. Alison Martin. New York: Routledge, 1993.

———. *Speculum of the Other Woman.* Trans. Gillian C. Gill. Ithaca, NY: Cornell University Press, 1985.

———. *This Sex Which Is Not One.* Trans. Catherine Porter with Carolyn Burke. Ithaca, NY: Cornell University Press, 1985.

Johnson, Barbara. "Translator's Introduction." In Jacques Derrida, *Dissemination.* London: Athlone Press, 1981, vii–ix.

Keen, David. *The Benefits of Famine: A Political Economy of Famine and Relief in Southwestern Sudan, 1983–1989.* Princeton, NJ: Princeton University Press, 1994.

Keen, David, and Ken Wilson. "Engaging with Violence: A Reassessment of Relief in Wartime." In *War and Hunger: Rethinking International Responses to Complex Emergencies,* ed. Joanna Macrae and Anthony Zwi. London: Zed Books, 1994, 209–221.

Kristeva, Julia. "La Femme, ce n'est jamais ça." *Tel quel* 59 (1974): 20–21. Partial translation as "Woman Cannot Be Defined." *New French Feminisms,* ed. Elaine Marks and Isabelle de Courtivron. Amherst: University of Massachusetts Press, 1980, 137–138.

———. *Revolution in Poetic Language.* Trans. Margaret Waller. New York: Columbia University Press, 1984.

———. *Strangers to Ourselves.* Trans. Leon S. Roudiez. New York: Columbia University Press, 1991.

Lacan, Jacques. *Écrits: A Selection.* Trans. Alan Sheridan. London: Routledge, 1980.

Laclau, Ernesto. "Preface" to Slavoj Zizek, *The Sublime Object of Ideology.* London: Verso, 1989, ix–xv.

Laclau, Ernesto, ed. *New Reflections on the Revolution of Our Time.* London: Verso, 1990.

———. *Politics and Ideology in Marxist Theory.* Oxford: Blackwell, 1979.

Laclau, Ernesto, and Chantal Mouffe. *Hegemony and Socialist Strategy: Towards a Radical Democratic Politics.* London: Verso, 1985.

Laclau, Ernesto, and Lilian Zac. "Minding the Gap: The Subject of Politics." In *The Making of Political Identities,* ed. Ernesto Laclau. London: Verso, 1994, 11–39.

Lacoue-Labarthe, Philippe. *Heidegger, Art and Politics: The Fiction of the Political.* Trans. Chris Turner. Oxford: Blackwell, 1990.

Larrain, Jorge. *The Concept of Ideology.* London: Hutchinson, 1979.

Lefort, Claude. *Democracy and Political Theory.* Trans. David Macey. Cambridge: Polity, 1988.

———. *The Political Forms of Modern Society.* Trans. John B. Thompson. Cambridge: Polity, 1986.

Macey, David. "Introduction." In *The Four Fundamental Concepts of Psychoanalysis,* ed. Jacques Lacan. Harmondsworth, UK: Penguin, 1994, vii–xxxviii.

Madden, Jenny, and Ben Seymour. "Terrible Old Stalinist with the Answer to Life, the Universe and Everything." *Real Life, Independent on Sunday,* 21 June 1998.

Marx, Karl. "Preface to 'A Critique of Political Economy.'" In *Karl Marx: Selected Writings,* ed. David McLellan. Oxford: Oxford University Press, 1977, 388–391.

Marx, Karl, and Frederick Engels. "The Communist Manifesto Party." In *Karl Marx: Selected Writings,* ed. David McLellan. Oxford: Oxford University Press, 1977, 221–247.

McLellan, David. *Ideology.* 2nd ed. Buckingham, UK: Open University Press, 1995.

McNay, Lois. *Foucault and Feminism: Power, Gender and the Self.* Cambridge: Polity, 1992.

Mitchell, Juliet. *Psychoanalysis and Feminism.* Harmondsworth, UK: Penguin, 1974.

Mitchell, Juliet, and Jacqueline Rose. *Feminine Sexuality: Jacques Lacan and the École Freudienne.* Trans. Jacqueline Rose. New York: Norton, 1985.

Morley, David, and Kuan-Hsing Chen, eds. *Stuart Hall: Critical Dialogues in Cultural Studies.* London: Routledge, 1996.

Moss, Jeremy, ed. *The Later Foucault: Politics and Philosophy.* London: Sage, 1998.

Muller, John P., and William J. Richardson. *Lacan and Language: A Reader's Guide to Écrits.* New York: International Universities Press, 1982.

Norval, Aletta. "Letter to Ernesto." In *New Reflections on the Revolution of Our Time,* ed. Ernesto Laclau. London: Verso, 1990, 135–157.

Rabinow, Paul, ed. *The Foucault Reader.* New York: Random House, 1984.

Rae, Alastair I. M. *Quantum Physics: Illusion or Reality?* Cambridge: Cambridge University Press, 1986.

Salecl, Renata. *The Spoils of Freedom: Psychoanalysis and Feminism After the Fall of Socialism.* London: Routledge, 1994.

Saussure, Ferdinand de. *Course in General Linguistics.* Trans. Wade Baskin. New York: McGraw-Hill, 1966.

Sheridan, Alan. *Michel Foucault: The Will to Truth.* London: Tavistock, 1980.

Staten, Henry. *Wittgenstein and Derrida.* Oxford: Basil Blackwell, 1984.

Vološinov, V. N. *Marxism and the Philosophy of Language.* Trans. Ladislav Matejka and I. R. Titunik. Cambridge: Harvard University Press, 1986.

Waever, Ole. "Securitization and Desecuritization." In *On Security,* ed. Ronnie D. Lipschutz. New York: Columbia University Press, 1995, 46–86.

Walker, R. B. J. *Inside/Outside: International Relations as Political Theory.* Cambridge: Cambridge University Press, 1993.

Weber, Max. "Politics as a Vocation." In *From Max Weber: Essays in Sociology,* ed. and trans. H. H. Gerth and C. Wright Mills. London: Routledge, 1948.

———. *The Theory of Social and Economic Organization.* Trans. A. M. Henderson and Talcott Parsons. New York: Free Press, 1947.

Wright, Elizabeth, and Edmond Wright. *The Žižek Reader.* Oxford: Blackwell, 1999.

Žižek, Slavoj. "Beyond Discourse Analysis." In *New Reflections on the Revolution of our Time,* ed. Ernesto Laclau. London: Verso, 1990, 249–260.

———. *Enjoy Your Symptom: Jacques Lacan in Hollywood and Out.* New York: Routledge, 1992.

———. *For They Know Not What They Do: Enjoyment as a Political Factor.* London: Verso, 1991.

———. *The Indivisible Remainder: An Essay on Schelling and Related Matters.* London: Verso, 1996.

———. *Looking Awry: An Introduction to Jacques Lacan through Popular Culture.* Cambridge, MA: MIT Press, 1991.

———. *The Metastases of Enjoyment: Six Essays on Women and Causality.* London: Verso, 1994.

———. *The Plague of Fantasies.* London: Verso, 1997.

———. *The Sublime Object of Ideology.* London: Verso, 1989.

———. *Tarrying with the Negative: Kant, Hegel and the Critique of Ideology.* Durham, NC: Duke University Press, 1993.

———, ed. *Everything You Always Wanted to Know About Lacan (But Were Afraid to Ask Hitchcock).* London: Verso, 1992.

———, ed. *Mapping Ideology.* London: Verso, 1994.

Žižek, Slavoj, and Renata Salecl. "Lacan in Slovenia." In *A Critical Sense: Interviews with Intellectuals,* ed. Peter Osborne. London: Routledge, 1996, 21–46.

Index

absence, 75–76. *See also* concealment; lack; presence
accident, 71, 77
act: political, 8, 137, 141. *See also* Laclau; lack; Žižek
activism, 57
actualité. *See* present
Althusser, Louis, 35, 131
always: already, 82, 94, 119; to come, 83. *See also* retrospective
analysis: deconstruction as, 73; of discourse, 54, 119; political, 3; of power, 52–56
anatomo-politics, 48–52, 54. *See also* biopolitics
antagonism, 5, 89, 113, 116, 133; constitutive, 120; fundamental, 117; social, 111, 136. *See also* Real; repression
archeology, 42, 44. *See also* Foucault
arrow in flight, 67. *See also* presence
articulation, 126–127, 131, 132–133. *See also* practice; rearticulation
as if, 115. *See also* performative
Austin, J. L., 75–78
authority, 81; discourse, 13; symbolic, 114; Weber's distinction, 4
axes. *See* genealogy

backward. *See* retrospective
Barthes, Roland, 25–26
being: of language, 96. *See also* subject
belief, 115
Bhabha, Homi, 129–130

big Other. *See* symbolic order
binaries. *See* hierarchies
biopolitics, 54. *See also* anatomo-politics; body
blood, 55
body: docile 51–52; image, 90; materiality of, 32–33; and power, 55; sexed, 31. *See also* biopolitics
Butler, Judith, 32–33
Buzan, Barry, 11

calculable, 13. *See also* depoliticization; incalculable; technologization
capitalism, 54–55
cause. *See* origin
class, 127, 128; consciousness, 36; and ideas 35; struggle, 131
closed system, 132, 134
closure: lack of, 133
communication, 75–76
community: fictional, 6; political, 6, 139
complementary, 141
complex emergency, 10
concealment: and critique of ideology, 118; of lack, 101, 138; of origin, 5, 8; and production, 102. *See also* absence; depoliticization; dividing practices; naturalize; normalization; technologization
conflict, 75. *See also* crisis; tension
conscious. *See under* unconscious
consciousness, 34; class, 36 false, 36, 130. *See also* class; ideology

155

About the Book

Offering a sophisticated introduction to the major poststructuralist thinkers, this book shows how Foucault, Derrida, Lacan, and Žižek can help us expose the depoliticization found in conventional international relations theory.

Edkins argues that contrary to the opinions of their detractors, the poststructuralists *are* concerned with the big questions of international politics: It is precisely their work that analyzes the political and explains the processes of depoliticization and technologization. Paying particular attention to notions of the subject and subjectivity in relation to the political, and to the relationship between ideology and social reality, Edkins explores, in short, why Foucault and others matter for international relations.

Jenny Edkins is lecturer in the Department of International Politics at the University of Wales, Aberystwyth. She is coeditor of *Sovereignty and Subjectivity* and author of *Famines and Modernity: Pictures of Hunger, Concepts of Famine, Practices of Aid.*